D1125526

David Scott's Guide to Managing Credit and Debt

David L. Scott

Professor of Accounting and Finance

Valdosta State University

Houghton Mifflin Company
Boston • New York

This publication is designed to provide accurate and authoritative information in regard to the subject matter covered. It is sold with the understanding that neither the author nor the Publisher is engaged in rendering legal, accounting, or other professional advice with respect to this publication. If, as a direct result of information supplied through this publication, legal advice or other expert assistance is required, the services of a competent professional person should be sought.

Visit our website: www.houghtonmifflinbooks.com

Library of Congress Cataloging-in-Publication Data
Scott, David Logan, 1942-
  David Scott's guide to managing credit and debt / David L. Scott.-- 1st ed.
      p. cm.
  Includes index.
  ISBN-13: 978-0-618-45870-7
  ISBN-10: 0-618-45870-0
  1. Finance, Personal. 2. Consumer credit. 3. Debt. I. Title: Guide to managing credit and debt. II. Title.
  HG179.S368 2005
  332.024'02--dc22

                                    2004027761

Manufactured in the United States of America.

Book design by Joyce C. Weston.
Data in Figure 25, page 94, courtesy of American Bankruptcy Institute.

QUM 10 9 8 7 6 5 4 3 2 1

David Scott's Guide to
Managing Credit and Debt

Contents

Introduction

People who are sufficiently wealthy aren't likely to spend a lot of time worrying about managing their credit, because they have little need to borrow money. And if they do have outstanding loans, plenty of cash and assets are generally available to cover the required payments. Some people are in this situation, but not many, and probably not you. If you are typical, you probably have a car loan, home loan, credit card balances, and, maybe, some personal loans. Many individuals and families struggle with debt that is continuously rolled forward, month after month, and year after year. In the worst cases, debt moved into future months is like a rolling snowball that becomes ever bigger and more difficult to manage. Hopefully, you are not in this situation either. Credit abuse can ruin the quality of your life. Persistent credit difficulties are a cause of sleepless nights, deteriorating health, and failed personal relationships. Bad finances have caused more than a few marriages to go sour.

Life doesn't have to end up like this. It is possible to gain control of your finances, even if you have been a chronic credit abuser. The cure isn't easy, and it certainly isn't painless. People who end up with credit difficulties are generally unable to control their impulse to spend. Failing to control spending means you are likely to experience credit difficulties no matter how much income you earn. An understanding of where and how to shop for credit is important, of course, because it permits you to save on finance charges. But saving on finance charges will be like spitting in the wind if your debts grow so large that you must secure additional loans in order to keep current on your existing debt.

This book offers no magic solutions for solving debt problems. If your debts have reached the point where you are experiencing difficulty coming up with the required payments to your creditors, there is little choice other than to suffer the pain of reducing the amount of money you spend. Spending is like eating: too much of either will produce unpleasant results. Credit management means more than spending less, however. Understanding how interest is calculated and where to look for the best deals on credit can go a long way toward helping you manage your credit intelligently. Similarly, determining where your money is going between paychecks can often allow you to cut back without feeling a lot of pain. Simply getting your financial house in order and paying attention to details will lead to more intelligent credit management.

After reading this book you should have a better understanding of

- the importance of a personal budget in managing your finances;
- the manner in which government policy affects the interest rates you pay to borrow money;
- how economic forecasts affect interest rates;
- the most appropriate lenders to approach for various kinds of loans;
- how best to prepare when you will be seeking a loan;
- how to compare interest rate quotations from different lenders;
- what factors to look for and avoid in a credit card;
- why your credit record is important; and
- how to negotiate with your creditors.

The major factors in intelligent debt management are self-discipline and applying common sense to financial matters. It should be obvious that buying a new car at a time when you are having difficulty making payments on your credit cards may send your finances over the edge. Still, many consumers do borrow to purchase things they don't need while they are struggling to make the payments on their current debt. If this sounds familiar, read on.

David L. Scott
Valdosta, Georgia

1 The Good and the Bad of Credit

Borrowing involves obtaining goods, services, or a sum of money in return for a promise of future repayment. Loans can originate with the supplier of a good or service (e.g., a business that sells you something and allows you to pay later) or with a third party (e.g., a bank or credit union that lends you money). Borrowing results from a decision you make to buy now and pay later. If you opt not to purchase a good or service a little at a time (e.g., buy one piece of bedroom furniture each month) or save until you have sufficient funds to pay in full, borrowing allows you to acquire and enjoy a good or service in return for agreeing to make a future payment or series of payments.

The availability and utilization of credit have a major impact on the domestic and international economy. Increased credit availability and an accompanying reduction in interest rates influence businesses and individuals to increase both their borrowing and spending. Low interest rates stimulate home building, automobile sales, and business spending for new equipment, all of which cause businesses to expand output and hire additional workers as they attempt to increase revenues and profits. In short, increased credit availability tends to spur the economy.

Federal authorities regularly take steps to influence credit availability in an attempt to affect economic activity. Politicians and federal regulators concerned about high unemployment, reduced business investment spending, and deteriorating economic activity work to increase the availability of credit, especially prior to an election. A vibrant economy makes for happy voters and a more likely reelection of incumbents. The opposite policies are implemented to restrict credit growth when the economy is operating near full capacity and inflation is a concern. Reduced credit availability and the accompanying increase in interest rates have a negative influence on lending and economic activity.

The Good, the Bad, and the Ugly of Credit Use and Abuse

Buying on credit isn't financially unsound or ethically wrong, as long as you don't borrow to excess and as long as borrowed money isn't squandered on unneeded goods and services that you would ordinarily forgo. The availability of credit has become an important consideration in making a decision on many large purchases. Most families would be unable to enjoy living in their own home if real estate purchases were made only for cash. Businesses routinely use borrowed funds to help pay for inventories, new equipment, and factories, and to provide financing for acquisitions and internal improvements that increase their efficiency and competitiveness. Most businesses would find it difficult to grow and compete if credit were unavailable.

Borrowers' need for additional funds benefits individuals and companies that hold excess funds. These savers are offered an opportunity to earn investment income on money that would otherwise remain idle. Excess funds of savers sometimes find their way directly to borrowers. Businesses that have extra funds often lend money directly to other businesses that are in need of funds for investment. Likewise, individual investors may funnel their savings to businesses and governments by purchasing newly issued debt securities. Individuals ordinarily make their extra monies accessible to borrowers by depositing the funds in financial intermediaries (e.g., banks, credit unions, and savings and loan associations) that, in turn, lend the funds to families and businesses needing additional monies. The bottom line is credit availability sustains a great many businesses and jobs at the same time that it offers a more pleasant life for individuals and families who have the financial discipline to use this source of money intelligently.

On the negative side, interest charges on borrowed funds have the effect of increasing the cost of goods and services that are purchased on credit. Individuals, businesses, and governments sometimes borrow to excess, especially when credit is cheap and readily available. Excessive use of credit can cause a borrower to incur such large financial obligations that insufficient funds are available for normal spending needs. Unrestrained borrowing has been a cause of stress, broken marriages, bankrupt companies, and insolvent governments unable to pay for essential services.

> **Tip**
>
> Think twice about cosigning a loan and guaranteeing someone else's debt, a goodwill action on your part that can result in several bad consequences. First, you will have to pay if the borrower doesn't. You may also be responsible for late fees or collection costs, which increase the amount for which you are liable. You are also subject to being sued or having your wages garnished, and a default may be reflected in your credit record.

Potential Advantages of Credit Use

1. *Credit allows you to readily acquire and enjoy the use of expensive items.* To a large extent, borrowing is used to acquire assets that provide years of use or enjoyment. Purchasing a new vehicle with borrowed money permits you to enjoy ownership of the vehicle during the years you repay the loan. When the loan is fully repaid in three, four, or five years, you will own the vehicle free and clear of debt. Depending on the vehicle's condition and your own desire for a newer model, you will have the option to trade for something newer or drive the vehicle a few more years. The borrow-and-buy cycle will then begin again. Without the availability of credit, you would have to save over many months or years in order to be able to acquire expensive items such as an automobile or truck.

2. *Credit availability provides you with an emergency source of funds.* What would you do if your vehicle broke down and, because you didn't have sufficient funds to pay for the required repairs, left you stranded in a distant town? How would you handle it if your home's furnace gave out during the winter and you were short of savings to pay for a replacement? Nearly everyone encounters situations in which insufficient money is available to take care of some pressing need. Credit provides you with the ability to obtain, on relatively short notice, the money that is required to bridge a temporary shortage of funds.

3. *Borrowing can result in tax savings.* Interest paid on certain types of loans can be used as a deduction in calculating your taxable income and income tax liability. Individual taxpayers are permitted to deduct the interest paid on loans used to buy first and second homes (motor homes and boats sometimes

also qualify). Likewise, interest charges resulting from borrowing funds that are used to acquire certain income-producing investments are generally deductible in calculating taxable income and income taxes. Interest paid by individuals on most consumer loans and credit card balances is not permitted as a tax deduction. A business is permitted to deduct nearly all its interest expenses when calculating its income tax liability. Governments collect rather than pay taxes, and so they are on the opposite side of tax deductions and would benefit from additional tax revenues if individuals and businesses were not permitted to deduct interest expenses.

4. *Credit allows you to make a purchase prior to a price increase.* You may have decided to purchase a particular item that you anticipate will soon increase in price. Perhaps you have been thinking about buying a house, jewelry, fuel oil, wallpaper, or any of a million other things. Rather than wait until you are able to accumulate sufficient funds to make the purchase at the higher price, credit availability permits you to use borrowed money to make the purchase prior to the price increase. For example, you may have read in the newspaper that there will soon be a $700 increase in the manufacturer's suggested retail price of an automobile you have been planning to purchase. You may be better off buying now, at the current price, even though an earlier purchase will cause you to have to borrow a portion of the current purchase price. Being able to acquire a product prior to a price increase is especially beneficial during periods of high inflation, when price increases can be substantial.

5. *Credit availability offers convenience.* It is frequently more convenient to pay for a good or service by using a credit source rather than paying with cash. Ordering products on the tele-

phone or online via a computer nearly always requires that you have access to a credit card. The alternative of mailing a check may cause you to wait weeks until the seller is assured the bank will honor your check. Credit cards are virtually mandatory for certain transactions, such as renting a vehicle or guaranteeing hotel room reservations.

6. *Certain credit sources permit you to pay later without being charged interest.* Being able to delay payment for a good or service without being charged a fee is to your advantage because it allows you to retain control over your money for a longer period of time. This means you are able to use someone else's money without charge at the same time you can continue to earn interest on your own money. Credit card issuers often allow users up to 40 or 50 days to pay for a purchase without incurring any fees or interest charges. Some retailers, especially furniture stores, offer customers the opportunity to make delayed payments without incurring interest charges. It is to your advantage to delay paying for a purchase for as long as possible so long as you aren't charged any interest or fees for the money that is borrowed.

7. *Credit allows you to travel or shop without being required to carry large amounts of cash.* Maintaining large amounts of cash in your possession subjects you to the risk that the money will be lost or stolen. Carrying cash also makes it more likely that

---

Tip

Compared to loans with a fixed interest rate, loans with a variable interest rate entail more risk for a borrower. A variable interest rate can result in changing payments to the lender over time. Small loan payments in the early months may turn into large loan payments in the later months.

you will be subject to a mugging. Traveler's checks are an alternative to cash or credit cards, but they are sometimes inconvenient to buy and their purchase may entail a fee. Carrying cash or traveler's checks (as opposed to a credit card) keeps you from earning interest on these funds. Buying $2,000 in traveler's checks means you have $2,000 less that is invested and producing income.

8. *Buying on credit allows you to use someone else's money while you retain control over your own funds.* Credit allows you to acquire goods and services without having to deplete your own funds. Perhaps your funds are profitably invested at a time when you need to purchase new clothing or trade cars. Borrowing makes it possible to acquire whatever it is that you need while your funds remain fully invested. Of course, this is an advantage only when your funds are expected to earn a return that is higher than the rate you are paying a creditor. Paying a creditor 8 percent interest at the same time your own savings are earning 2 percent isn't a great idea.

9. *Lenders sometimes offer borrowers special benefits at no additional cost.* Competition among creditors, especially issuers of credit cards, has caused lenders to offer customers a variety of benefits, often without charge. Credit card issuers often provide cardholders with airline frequent-flier points (generally one point per dollar charged), hotel stays, cash rebates, liability coverage on rental car damage, warranty extensions on purchased goods, specialized life insurance coverage, and so forth. These perks are generally available without charge on certain cards.

10. *Paying by credit card creates a helpful spending record.* Detailed monthly credit card statements are valuable sources of information for those who wish to maintain a record of their spending. For example, someone wishing to undertake a

personal budget can review past credit card statements to determine how money has been spent. Some credit card issuers provide a year-end record of annual charges grouped into spending categories, which can be particularly helpful for providing an overview of how you have used your money.

11. *Credit purchases often provide leverage in the event a problem develops with your purchase.* Pay cash for a purchase and you have little clout if something goes wrong with the transaction or with the item or service you purchased. Once it has your money, a business may have little incentive to make certain you are satisfied with a purchase. On the other hand, owing money to a merchant who fears you might decide not to pay places you in a better position to push for a satisfactory solution to any problem that develops. This leverage is particularly important when you make a purchase over the telephone or the Internet.

Potential Disadvantages of Credit Use

1. *Credit availability makes it convenient to buy goods and services that ordinarily would not be purchased.* Credit provides increased buying power that many individuals, families, and institutions find difficult to hold in check. Goods and services that would ordinarily remain on the shelf are more likely to be acquired and consumed when sufficient credit is available. If the cash isn't available and credit isn't an option, you will be unable to purchase something. Even when you do have the cash, paying with real money makes it more evident that making that particular purchase means you will have less (or no) money available for something else. Paying for purchases with borrowed money short circuits the financial discipline that is often imposed by cash.

2. *Borrowing generally increases the cost of a good or service.* Fees and interest that are charged by lenders result in a higher cost for goods and services that are purchased with borrowed money. The sum of all the payments you make on an automobile loan might amount to $22,000, when you could have purchased the vehicle for a cash price of $17,500. The higher the interest rate and the longer a loan's term, the more that credit adds to the cost of a purchase. Lenders frequently impose additional fees for originating a loan, for late payments, and for prepaying a loan (repaying prior to the scheduled maturity).

Figure 1 illustrates the cost of credit use for three common types of loans: personal, vehicle, and home. As is typical for most consumer borrowing, the loans are amortized with equal monthly payments comprised partly of interest and partly of principal. The first example is a $1,500 personal loan, shown with different terms and interest rates. Typically, a personal loan is unsecured (e.g., no collateral is pledged), and proceeds may be used for a vacation, to pay down credit card balances, or to take care of a medical bill. The 2-year personal loan with a 9 percent interest rate requires 24 monthly payments of $68.53 and results in paying $144.72 more than the amount borrowed. This is the interest cost of the loan, and it represents the additional cost of buying on credit rather than with cash. The same loan for 3 years has an overall interest cost of $217.20. The cost of credit for a 25-year home loan of $110,000 is mind-numbing. At an interest rate of 7 percent, this 25-year home loan results in the borrower paying the lender a total of $233,238, including $123,238 in interest.

As you would expect, monthly payments are higher the shorter the term of the loan. Repaying a loan more quickly

Figure 1 ■ The Cost of Using Credit

Personal loan of $1,500

Term	Monthly Payment	Total of Payments	Cost of Credit	Monthly Payment	Total of Payments	Cost of Credit
	7% Interest			**9% Interest**		
1 year	$129.79	$1,557.48	$ 57.48	$131.18	$1,574.16	$ 74.16
2 years	67.16	1,611.84	111.84	68.53	1,644.72	144.72
3 years	46.32	1,667.52	167.52	47.70	1,717.20	217.20

Vehicle loan of $18,000

Term	Monthly Payment	Total of Payments	Cost of Credit	Monthly Payment	Total of Payments	Cost of Credit
	5.5% Interest			**7.5% Interest**		
3 years	$543.53	$19,567.08	$1,567.08	$559.91	$20,156.76	$2,156.76
4 years	416.62	19,997.76	1,997.76	435.22	20,890.56	2,890.56
5 years	343.82	20,629.20	2,629.20	360.68	21,640.80	3,640.80
6 years	294.08	21,173.76	3,173.76	311.22	22,407.84	4,407.84

Home loan of $110,000

Term	Monthly Payment	Total of Payments	Cost of Credit	Monthly Payment	Total of Payments	Cost of Credit
	5.5% Interest			**7% Interest**		
15 years	$898.75	$161,775	$51,775	$988.71	$177,968	$ 67,968
20 years	756.68	181,603	71,603	852.83	204,679	94,679
25 years	675.50	202,650	92,650	777.46	233,238	123,238

means you must pay more each month toward the principal, thereby reducing the principal amount on which interest is charged. A 15-year home loan of $110,000 at a 7 percent interest rate requires monthly payments of $988.71, while extending the term of the loan to 25 years results in a monthly payment reduction of approximately $210, to $777.46. Although each of the payments is smaller in size, you must make 120 additional payments that result in a greater total amount of money being paid to the lender. Notice the difference in interest cost between a 3-year and 6-year $18,000 vehicle loan. At an interest rate of 5.5 percent, a borrower will pay over $1,600 in additional interest expense when the $18,000 loan is extended by three years.

3. *Credit availability results in many individuals and businesses becoming mired in debt.* Individuals and businesses sometimes borrow such a large amount of money that they end up struggling to make payments on their loans. In the worst case, borrowers are unable to remain current on their loan obligations. Personal and corporate bankruptcies increased dramatically in the last decade as borrowers found it necessary or, in some cases, convenient, to escape their financial obligations. More than a few marriages have collapsed because of financial problems resulting from credit abuse.

4. *Frequent credit use allows lenders to monitor your spending habits.* The more purchases you charge, the more data about your spending activities creditors and merchants are able to accumulate. Cash payments for goods and services don't produce a paper or electronic trail that allows others to learn how you have been spending your money.

Tip If you decide to cosign a loan, ask the lender to agree, in writing, to notify you if the borrower misses a payment. Early notice will allow you time to deal with the problem and make back payments without being required to repay the entire balance of the loan.

Tip Make it a goal to be free of debt by the time you expect to retire. Choose a home loan and vehicle loans that you expect to be able to repay during your working years. It is difficult to enjoy retirement when you are required to worry about how your creditors are to be paid.

5. *Using credit makes it more likely that criminals will steal your identity.* Identity theft has become an increasing problem for individuals, especially those who hold credit cards. Criminals are unlikely to steal your identity, or even have an interest in stealing your identity, if you never borrow. After all, identity theft generally occurs because criminals want to charge goods and services in your name.

Don't assume that just because the listed number of advantages is greater than the listed number of disadvantages that borrowing is the preferred method of paying for goods and services. Borrowing has the potential to cause severe financial problems that can wreck someone's life. Individuals without the discipline to control borrowing are often better off avoiding credit use altogether (other than for the purchase of a home).

Why Borrow?

Individuals, businesses, and governments borrow for several reasons. Most important by far is the fact that individuals and organizations frequently don't have sufficient funds to pay in full for purchases they are unable or unwilling to put off. Some purchases entail a substantial expense that would normally be impossible without using borrowed money. Individuals borrow to buy homes, businesses borrow to buy factories, and govern-

Figure 2 ■ Net Borrowing in U.S. Credit Markets, 1985–2003

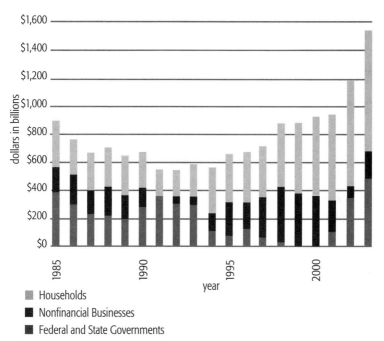

ments borrow to build highways. Borrowers sometimes make a decision to avoid dipping into their savings even though sufficient funds are available to pay in full for their purchases. For example, a family with substantial savings may decide to borrow most of the purchase price of a new automobile. Figure 2 offers a look at the immense amounts of money borrowed each year by domestic governments, businesses, and households.

Business Borrowing

Businesses are typically financed with a combination of borrowed money, ownership contributions, and funds that have been retained from profits. Borrowing provides businesses with an alternative source of capital to purchase additional productive assets (e.g., machinery and buildings) and to finance ongoing operations. Financing a firm's expansion with credit allows the existing owners to avoid bringing in additional investors who would share in the profits. Borrowing can be used to pay for an expansion that will increase the return earned on the owners' investment.

Businesses have an incentive to utilize borrowing because the interest that is paid to lenders can be deducted from income when the businesses calculate their federal and state income taxes. The reduced taxes resulting from interest expense cause many businesses to favor borrowing over issuing additional shares of ownership, on which dividends must be paid with after-tax income. In other words, distributing profits to owners does not result in a tax deduction for a business.

A substantial amount of long-term business borrowing stipulates a fixed interest rate that permits a business to establish a constant outflow of cash for an extended period of time. Businesses often borrow millions of dollars at a fixed rate of interest for terms of 25 years or longer. This financial arrangement permits a borrower to determine exactly how many dollars will be required each month or each year to keep a loan current. Businesses frequently have an option to borrow at a variable rate of interest, especially on short-term loans. Loans with variable interest rates do not fix a firm's cost of funds.

The financing mix between owner contributions and borrowed money varies from industry to industry and from firm to firm. Companies that enjoy relatively stable revenues (predictable sales that do not fluctuate much from quarter to quarter and year to year) are better able to cope with the fixed payments normally required of borrowers. The managers of an electric utility are generally able to forecast the firm's revenues with reasonable accuracy, thereby allowing these firms to utilize substantial amounts of debt to pay for the purchases of generating plants, transmission facilities, and fuel. On the other hand, businesses such as steel manufacturers and mining companies have fluctuating revenues that are difficult to forecast accurately. These firms are more at risk when large amounts of debt are used to finance the firm's assets. Companies with fluctuating revenues and substantial amounts of debt will occasionally find it difficult to meet fixed interest and principal payments, especially during a period of weak business activity.

Government Borrowing

Governments borrow when tax and fee collections are insufficient to meet spending requirements. Governments at all levels have increasingly relied on borrowed funds to pay for supplying the goods and services their citizens have demanded. Although governments can reduce their reliance on borrowing by reining in spending and/or by increasing taxes, neither option is appealing to lawmakers, who rely on the votes and campaign contributions of taxpayers and recipients of government services and contracts. Citizens lobby to keep open nearby military installations and the elderly rail against reductions in Medicare and Social Security payments at the same time that nearly all voters cry "no new taxes." Everyone wants criminals in prison, but taxpayers often seem unwilling to pay the full cost of their incarceration. Figure 3 illustrates the giant increase in the federal debt since 1970. Note that the amount of debt actually declined for several years in the late 1990s and early 2000s when the U.S. government operated at a surplus. However, this was the exception rather than the rule.

A substantial amount of government spending is devoted to the construction or acquisition of long-lasting assets such as bridges, monuments, buildings, and equipment. Anticipated life

Figure 3 ■ Publicly Held Federal Debt

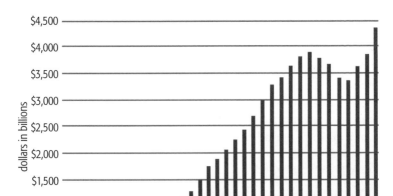

spans of 20 or 30 years or even longer make it relatively easy to accept that at least a portion of these assets should be financed with borrowed money—an alternative that allows citizens to enjoy the benefits of the assets at the same time that payments are being made on the loans. Local citizens derive long-lasting benefits from a new school or recreation complex, and vehicle owners can be expected to enjoy many years of benefits from an improved road system. Of course, governments at all levels have become involved with their share of boondoggles, including unneeded highway interchanges, airport renovations, and sports stadiums.

Government borrowing to support services and short-term assets that are consumed long before loans are repaid is more worrisome. Borrowing to pay for current social programs, especially programs that can be expected to require even larger financial commitments in future years, presents a major problem with long-term consequences. Financing short-term government spending requirements with long-term debt commitments (including short-term loans that must be continually renewed) can present long-term financial difficulties because citizens will be stuck with interest and principal payments long after the government expenditures have been made and benefits have been exhausted. Long-term borrowing to support short-term spending requirements causes future generations of citizens to pay for the excesses of their parents and grandparents who consumed government resources beyond their willingness to pay the full cost of those resources. Unlike corporate and individual borrowing, a substantial amount of government borrowing takes place with the full intent to buy and consume now while letting someone else pay later.

Personal Borrowing

Personal borrowing results when an individual is unable to pay for a purchase out of current income and either cannot or does not wish to tap savings. Individuals sometimes borrow directly from a seller (e.g., run a tab at a local hardware store or the doctor's office), but more often they become indebted to a third party such as a bank or credit union. An individual may use a credit card to purchase gasoline for the car, clothes for the kids, or medicine for family members. A family may arrange a credit union loan to purchase an automobile, acquire furniture for the house, or pay for a hospital stay. Individuals also borrow funds that are used to acquire investments or to repay outstanding loans (e.g., borrow from a bank or a credit union to pay off credit card balances or to refinance a home loan when interest rates have declined).

Tip Try not to use credit to buy things that are likely to be consumed before your loan repayments are complete. Continuing to pay for something that is no longer usable is a sign you are headed for financial difficulty.

While a major proportion of the money borrowed by businesses is used to purchase productive assets such as equipment and real estate that will produce revenues to repay the debt, and much government debt is incurred to pay for long-lasting assets (e.g., highways and buildings), personal debt is frequently used to facilitate the purchase of goods and services that are quickly consumed. There are exceptions, of course. Houses are long-lasting assets, and vehicles can have extended lives depending on how they are driven and maintained. Similarly, furniture and appliances can be expected to last several decades. Still, goods and services purchased by consumers with borrowed money are often long gone while the payments on the loans continue.

The Bottom Line of Credit Management

Credit has become an everyday necessity for governments, businesses, and most individuals. Credit permits governments to build schools, construct highways, and wage wars. Borrowing allows businesses to acquire equipment, build factories, and stock inventories. Credit helps individuals acquire homes, buy vehicles, and earn college diplomas. Unfortunately, credit can become addictive and be abused. Enjoyment now and payment later can be taken to the extreme. Governments abuse credit when politicians vote for popular spending programs but are afraid to levy the taxes necessary for adequate funding of these

Figure 4 ■ Internet Sites with Information on Credit Management

---

http://www.bankrate.com offers
- Current interest rates on mortgages, home equity loans, car loans, and credit cards.
- A calculator to figure payments for loans at different interest rates and maturity lengths.
- Advice on establishing a personal budget.
- General information about borrowing.

---

http://www.ftc.gov/ftc/consumer.htm offers
- Information on what to do about identity theft.
- Advice on financing an automobile.
- A listing of publications on credit reports, various types of loans, and credit regulations.

---

http://www.quickenloans.com offers
- Calculators for selecting or refinancing a loan.
- A primer on credit bureaus and credit reports.
- Information on evaluating refinancing a loan.

---

http://www.interest.com offers
- Information on current mortgage interest rates.
- A calculator to help make decisions on points, the amount you can afford to borrow, and monthly payments.
- Help on locating the lowest-cost mortgage loan.

---

http://money.cnn.com/pf/debt offers
- Educational information on controlling debt.
- Current offers on mortgages, credit cards, and car loans.
- News items related to borrowing.

---

http://credit.about.com offers
- A wide variety of information about credit.
- Links to related sites.

> **Tip** The Federal Trade Commission advises consumers to beware of companies that promise to fix your credit history or clean up your credit report. Often these firms are more interested in the money in your billfold than the information in your credit report.

programs. Businesses become greedy and abuse credit when they attempt to finance too large a proportion of their assets with money from lenders. Individuals abuse credit when they borrow in order to spend beyond their financial means. Credit use results in an improved lifestyle that can quickly deteriorate when borrowing is abused.

Figure 4 includes several Internet sites that offer information about credit. These sites will help keep you up to date on current interest rates and provide advice on how to compare various borrowing options. The Federal Trade Commission site at www.ftc.gov is particularly good for learning about safeguards that are available to borrowers. The Federal Trade Commission offers numerous publications of interest to borrowers. Read and learn about credit, because knowledge will allow you to make better financial decisions that result in a happier and more productive life.

2 Types and Sources of Consumer Credit

Not many years ago a borrower's alternatives were limited, in both the types of lenders that were actively making loans and the variety of loans that were available. Federal and state regulations limited the types of lending in which financial institutions could engage, and the Federal Reserve restricted the interest rates these institutions could legally pay to attract deposits. The upper limits on interest rates that could be paid on savings had the effect of artificially reducing the cost of money—both for financial institutions that held the deposits and for customers who borrowed from these institutions—below the level that would have existed in a free market. Financial deregulation during the 1970s and 1980s resulted in major changes that caused great turmoil in the financial markets. New players entered the lending game, and a dizzying array of innovative credit products were offered as new alternatives to borrowers.

Types of Consumer Credit

Loans come in a greater variety than crayons. Some loan agreements require that a borrower make a specified number of fixed monthly payments, each comprised of both interest and princi-

> **Tip** Beware of payday loans in which a postdated check is presented in exchange for money. The loan is to be repaid when funds are available on payday. Payday loans generally come with very high, double-digit interest rates. Borrowers who are unable to repay these loans are charged additional fees for an extension, putting them even deeper in debt.

pal, while other loans stipulate that you pay the lender a single sum on a predetermined date. Many lending agreements specify an interest rate that remains the same throughout the term of a loan, while other loans stipulate a variable interest rate that is periodically altered according to some identified standard. Some loans require that certain personal assets be pledged as collateral to be claimed by the lender in the event you default on the terms of the loan. Other loans are unsecured and granted on the basis of your promise of repayment. Loans with different maturities, different interest rates, different repayment plans, and different collateral requirements are offered by a bewildering array of lenders.

Installment Credit

Installment credit (also called *closed-end credit*) includes loans that require repayment of the amount borrowed in equal periodic payments, generally monthly. Loans written for the purchase of an automobile or a recreational vehicle are generally installment credit. This is also a popular method for financing the purchase of refrigerators, washing machines, and other high-end appliances. The lender will ordinarily retain the title (if one exists) to the asset being financed until the loan is completely repaid, at which time the title is relinquished to the borrower.

Perhaps you have decided to purchase a $22,000 automobile using personal savings of $4,000 combined with the proceeds of an $18,000 loan being offered through the dealer. The lender prepares a three-year loan agreement at 6 percent annual interest that requires that you make 36 monthly payments of $547.59. The loan will be paid off (i.e., have a zero balance) on the date of the last scheduled payment, at which time you will have a clear title to the automobile. The loan's repayment schedule is illustrated in Figure 5. The total amount paid in interest and fees equals the difference between the sum of all the payments that are made and the amount that is borrowed. In this example, you will pay a total of $19,713.24 over 36 months (36 months × $547.59 per month), which includes $1,713.38 in interest on the original principal of $18,000. Each $547.59 monthly payment to the lender is comprised partly of an interest charge and partly of a partial repayment of principal. The proportions of interest and principal change with each subsequent payment as the principal on the loan is gradually reduced. For example, Figure 5 shows that $90.00 of the first $547.59 payment goes toward interest; the first month's interest is calculated as one-twelfth of 6 percent times the $18,000 that is owed on the loan. The first payment of the third year (month 25) allocates $31.81 for interest and $515.78 to a reduction of principal; interest in the twenty-fifth month is less than in the first month because the outstanding balance on the loan has been reduced to $6,362.51.

Installment credit typically provides little flexibility for a borrower. An installment loan is specifically designed to finance a particular asset, and you do not have an option to arbitrarily disregard payments or to make payments of a size other than scheduled in the loan agreement. This doesn't mean you will go to jail or have all your personal assets confiscated if you miss a

Figure 5 ■ Payment Schedule for an Installment Loan

Month	Beginning Balance	Payment	Interest Paid	Principal Paid
1	$18,000.00	$547.59	$90.00	$457.59
2	17,542.41	547.59	87.71	459.88
3	17,082.53	547.59	85.41	462.16
4	16,620.37	547.59	83.10	464.49
5	16,155.88	547.59	80.78	466.82
6	16,689.06	547.59	78.45	469.15
7	15,219.91	547.59	76.10	471.50
8	14,748.41	547.59	73.74	473.85
9	14,274.56	547.59	71.37	476.22
10	13,798.34	547.59	68.99	478.60
11	13,319.74	547.59	66.60	481.00
12	12,838.74	547.59	64.19	483.40
13	12,355.34	547.59	61.78	485.82
14	11,869.52	547.59	59.35	488.25
15	11,381.27	547.59	56.91	490.69
16	10,890.58	547.59	54.45	493.14
17	10,397.44	547.59	51.99	495.61
18	9,901.83	547.59	49.51	498.09
19	9,403.74	547.59	47.02	500.58
20	8,903.16	547.59	44.52	503.06
21	8,400.10	547.59	42.00	505.59
22	7,894.51	547.59	39.47	508.12
23	7,386.39	547.59	36.93	510.66
24	6,875.73	547.59	34.38	513.22
25	6,362.51	547.59	31.81	515.78
26	5,846.73	547.59	29.23	518.36
27	5,328.37	547.59	26.64	520.95
28	4,807.42	547.59	24.04	523.56
29	4,383.86	547.59	21.42	526.18
30	3,757.68	547.59	18.79	528.81
31	3,228.87	547.59	16.14	531.45
32	2,697.42	547.59	13.49	534.11
33	2,163.31	547.59	10.82	536.78
34	1,626.53	547.59	8.13	539.46
35	1,087.01	547.59	5.44	542.16
36	544.91	547.59	2.68	544.91
Totals		$19,713.24	$1,713.38	$18,000.00

Note: Based on an $18,000 loan at 6% interest to be repaid in 36 monthly payments.

car payment. It does mean that you need to contact the lender in the event you will be unable to meet your scheduled payments.

Other Types of Consumer Credit

Noninstallment credit includes single-payment loans and loans that permit irregular payments and additional borrowing without submitting a new credit application. The latter category is also called *open-end credit*. Essentially, noninstallment credit applies to all forms of consumer credit other than fixed-payment loans, described in the previous section.

Single-payment loans, also called *term loans*, require that you repay on a specified date the entire amount that was borrowed. A term loan may require periodic interest payments, but more likely requires payment of accumulated interest at the same time the loan's principal is repaid. Suppose you borrow $5,000 for one year at 8 percent interest. At the end of the year, you repay the $5,000 plus the year's interest of $400 (8 percent of $5,000). If the term of the loan is less than one year, you will owe interest of less than $400, while a loan extending for more than a year will require interest of more than $400. Single-payment loans are useful if you expect to need the full amount borrowed for a specific length of time.

Open-end credit permits you to borrow more money as additional funds are needed, so long as the outstanding balance on the loan doesn't exceed a preestablished limit. Charge accounts and credit card accounts are the most common examples of open-end credit. Each type of account provides a continuous source of credit that is limited only by the maximum amount of credit stipulated in the lending agreement. You are permitted to diminish the debt by making payments and to add to the debt by borrowing additional sums without having to reapply for credit. Some types of open-end credit require that the entire debt be repaid on a particular date, although additional funds can be obtained so long as your cumulative borrowing hasn't exceeded an amount (your credit limit, or line of credit) specified in the loan agreement. Other types of open-end credit allow uneven, partial payments subject to a predetermined minimum established by the lender. The minimum payment may be a stipulated dollar amount (e.g., $10 per month) or a percentage (2 percent is common) of the outstanding balance. The following types of accounts are examples of open-end credit.

Charge account A charge account generally permits a borrower to avoid finance charges by paying the outstanding balance in full within a specified number of days following the closing date on the account's statement. An alternative is to make partial payments and incur interest charges on the balance. Charge accounts are popular among retailers (e.g., Target, Sears) that hope to both stimulate sales and generate interest income from customer accounts. Charge cards are also issued by businesses that desire to build customer loyalty (e.g., petroleum companies and airlines). Interest rates on charge accounts are generally quite high, making this an expensive source of credit unless you have the discipline and financial resources to repay the entire balance before it begins accruing interest. Charging purchases to your charge account generally makes it easier to return merchandise to the retailer that approved the account.

Credit card account Credit card accounts, such as those offered by Visa, MasterCard, Discover, and Optima, are the most popular form of open-end credit. Most individuals don't have just one credit card, they have a fistful of plastic. And while once it was large banks that mostly sponsored credit cards, now savings and loan associations, credit unions, brokerage firms, hotel chains,

> **Tip**
>
> Protect your checking account number as well as your credit card number. Scam artists will sometimes call and offer a deal in return for your reading all the numbers at the bottom of one of your checks. The telemarketer can use this checking account information for a demand draft that is processed much like a check. Your bank will deduct the amount of the draft from your checking account and pay the scam artist's bank.

automobile manufacturers, communications firms, and other organizations peddle their own branded cards through several financial firms that specialize in these credit accounts.

Credit cards can be used to purchase goods and services from merchants or to obtain cash from financial institutions and automated teller machines. Some card companies charge an annual fee of from $15 to $50 or more, while other cards are issued without an annual charge. Card companies typically permit cardholders to avoid interest charges when an account balance is paid in full by a prescribed date. A variety of methods are utilized to calculate interest charges on credit card accounts, a topic that is discussed in more detail in Chapter 6.

Personal line of credit A personal line of credit permits you to borrow funds as needed, generally by means of special checks supplied by the lender. The checks can be used to pay for goods and services, or they can be used to deposit funds to your regular checking account. A line of credit permits you to borrow and repay funds at your convenience, subject to a maximum amount that is specified at the time the loan is arranged. Interest charges are based on the outstanding loan balance and the length of time over which the funds are borrowed.

Home-equity loan A home-equity loan utilizes the equity in your home (i.e., the home's market value less the balance on any outstanding loans using the home as security) as collateral and can be structured either as a line of credit or as an installment loan. Home-equity loans are generally restricted to between 70 and 80 percent of a home's appraised value minus whatever amount is owed to a lender holding a first mortgage. Suppose you purchased a $100,000 home several years ago with a $25,000 down payment and a $75,000 loan. The home has now increased in value to $110,000, and the loan has been paid down to a current balance of $71,000. A home-equity loan of 75 percent would allow you to borrow a maximum of $11,500 (75 percent of $110,000 less the current $71,000 loan balance). Home-equity loans are a convenient (some critics say too convenient) form of borrowing at a competitive short-term interest rate. Once the paperwork is complete, you receive a book of checks to be used in any way you desire. Checks can be written for cash, to pay off other loans, or to purchase merchandise. An additional advantage is that, unlike most other types of consumer loans, interest paid on home-equity loans is allowed as an itemized deduction in calculating your federal income tax liability.

Individuals who lack the discipline to control their spending and borrowing are likely to abuse a home-equity loan. The availability of a large amount of borrowing power causes some people to spend more money, even if they have to borrow. Most home-equity loans specify a variable interest rate that can quickly swing upward, thereby causing the loan to become a greater financial burden. This variable interest rate makes a home-equity loan a ticking time bomb. Pledging your home as collateral for a loan places your primary residence at risk in the event you are unable to meet the required loan payments.

Travel and entertainment (T&E) account A T&E account, offered by American Express, Diners Club, and other financial services companies, provides credit for a prescribed period, generally 30 days, at which time charges must be paid in full. Credit is accessed by means of charge cards issued by the lender. A T&E account does not permit you to pay only a portion of your bill, as is allowed (actually encouraged) by credit card companies. Fewer retailers accept T&E cards compared with credit cards such as Visa and MasterCard; at the same time, T&E card issuers are more selective regarding the applicants whom they approve to receive their cards.

Thirty-day account and service credit Thirty-day accounts permit customers to defer payment for purchases by up to 30 days without incurring interest charges. Full payment is expected by the due date, and interest is not applicable for this type of account. Service credit, offered by utilities, doctors, and other suppliers of services, allows you to make payment within 15 to 30 days after a service is provided. For example, customers are perpetually in debt to the electric company, because payments for service always follow the usage of electricity. Both 30-day accounts and service credit are offered as a convenience to customers rather than as a money-making endeavor.

Sources of Credit

Specialized lenders were once the standard source of money for home loans, auto loans, and personal loans. You went to a savings and loan association for a real estate loan, you visited a commercial bank if you were interested in a loan for your business, you went to a commercial bank or a credit union if you needed a personal loan or an automobile loan, and you headed

> **Tip** Deregulation of financial institutions has allowed banks, savings and loan associations, and credit unions to expand into new areas of lending. It is worthwhile to shop for credit at several institutions and also at several types of institutions.

for a finance company if you were considered a poor credit risk or didn't know any better. Financial deregulation brought new lenders to the credit markets at the same time that it contributed to a blurring of the distinctions among the existing lenders. Savings and loan associations began making commercial and personal loans, and brokerage firms became aggressive real estate lenders. You can now use your home as collateral for a loan to purchase an automobile, borrow from your broker to pay for a vacation, and accumulate credits toward free airline trips by using your credit card.

Even though lenders are no longer as specialized as in years past, important differences remain among various financial institutions. Lenders vary in the qualifications they require of borrowers, the interest rates and fees they charge, the types of loans they make available, and the maturity lengths of loans they offer. Being better acquainted with various credit sources will help you determine which lenders are most likely to be sympathetic to your request for a loan. Figure 6 provides a summary of the various types of loans offered by the major providers of consumer credit.

Commercial Banks

Commercial banks generally offer a greater variety of loans than other lenders. Banks offer installment loans, term loans, and lines of credit on both a secured and an unsecured basis. Most

Figure 6 ■ Sources of Consumer Credit

Credit Source	Types of Loans	Features
Commercial banks	Installment loans Single-payment loans Credit card loans Second mortgages Education loans	High-quality loans Collateral often required Relatively low interest rates Preference for relatively large loans
Consumer finance companies	Installment loans Second mortgages	High interest rates Relatively small loans Low credit standards Quick decisions
Credit unions	Installment loans Second mortgages Credit card loans Education loans	Low interest rates Membership required Small loans Many unsecured loans
Life insurance companies	Loans against cash values	No required payments Relatively low interest rates No credit check required
Savings and loan associations	First mortgages Second mortgages Home improvement loans Installment loans Education loans	High-quality loans Collateral often required
Brokerage firms	Loans against securities	Brokerage account required Variable interest rate No required payments No credit check required Quick access to funds

> **Tip** You may be able to obtain a lower interest rate on a loan by agreeing to have loan payments automatically deducted from your checking or savings account. This option is certainly worth asking about. It may also save on late fees.

banks will make loans for the purpose of purchasing a boat, buying a home, taking a vacation, paying off another loan, investing in a business, fixing your roof, or paying your taxes. Commercial banks tend to be choosy lenders, concentrating on making loans to individuals and businesses with an established credit history. This cautious attitude is not universal, and many commercial banks are aggressive lenders. Overly aggressive banks sometimes find themselves with financial difficulties because large numbers of borrowers default on their obligations to the banks. Banks that concentrate on making high-quality loans suffer fewer losses to defaults and are generally able to offer competitive interest rates.

Savings and Loan Associations

Savings and loan associations (S&Ls) were long restricted to making commercial and residential real estate loans. Nearly all these loans carried long maturities and fixed interest rates. This was a conservative business that produced steady but relatively modest profits. Financial deregulation allowed these formerly specialized creditors to diversify their lending practices to the point where many larger S&Ls operate in a manner identical with that of commercial banks. Federal authorities permit S&Ls to make all types of commercial and personal loans. Despite the increased freedom, many S&Ls have continued to concentrate on making real estate loans and, to a lesser extent, vehicle loans.

Credit Unions

Credit unions are cooperative associations that accept savings from and make loans to individuals who have some affiliation, generally a common place of employment. Individuals who qualify for membership in a credit union must purchase a credit union share (e.g., make a small deposit of $5 or so) to activate their membership status and participate in the financial services that are offered. If your employer does not sponsor a credit union, you may qualify for membership in a nearby credit union. Credit unions tend to concentrate on making installment loans, especially loans for purchasing vehicles. Home-equity loans and unsecured personal loans are also offered by most credit unions. Larger credit unions make mortgage loans on residential real estate, although the maximum loan amount may be smaller than could be obtained at a commercial bank or S&L. Low overhead and expenses that are frequently partially subsidized by their sponsors often permit credit unions to offer loans at relatively low interest rates compared with those you would be required to pay at a commercial bank or S&L. Collection costs, slow repayments, and defaults are reduced at credit unions because they typically withhold loan payments from a borrower's paycheck. Volunteer work by members serves to further reduce the expenses incurred by credit unions.

Consumer Finance Companies

Consumer finance companies concentrate on writing installment loans and second mortgages. Loans that allow customers to repay other outstanding loans (borrow from Peter to pay Paul) are also popular offerings at consumer finance companies. Consumer finance companies are more willing to make relatively small loans, which commercial banks and S&Ls generally avoid. These lenders charge relatively high interest rates and are more likely than other lenders to approve loans for applicants with woeful credit histories or no prior borrowing experience. The worse an individual's credit history, the greater the amount of security a lender may require before approving a loan. Borrowers sometimes agree to pledge additional collateral in negotiating for reduced interest rates on loans.

High interest rates and excessive fees make consumer finance companies a relatively undesirable credit source. If you have unencumbered assets (i.e., assets that are not being used for collateral on another loan) and/or a history of responsible credit use, you can almost surely obtain a better deal on a loan at a commercial bank or an S&L than at a consumer finance company. Even if you don't consider yourself a particularly good credit risk, you should at least make an effort to talk with a bank when you are interested in borrowing money.

Sales Finance Companies

Sales finance companies are formed to lend money to customers of an affiliated company. For example, General Motors Acceptance Corporation (GMAC) acts as a credit source to car buyers at dealerships offering General Motors vehicles. GMAC borrows money in the financial markets and, in turn, lends it to consumers who purchase the firm's vehicles. Ford Credit performs the same function for Ford Motor Company. Sales

> **Tip** Beware of Internet sites that offer free credit reports. Some online operators set up high-tech sites as a way to capture your personal information that they may sell to others. Some fraudulent sites convince consumers to disclose credit card numbers, bank account information, Social Security numbers, and passwords.

finance companies periodically offer borrowers particularly attractive interest rates to stimulate business at the affiliated company. During 2002 and 2003 many purchasers of new vehicles were borrowing at zero percent interest. By charging zero interest, the auto companies were willing to lose money on financing vehicles in order to stimulate vehicle sales and, they hoped, earn a profit on the sales. These special rates are generally restricted to loans with a relatively short maturity (and high monthly payments) and to customers with a good credit rating. Without special financing, loans at sales finance companies are likely to be convenient, but more expensive than similar loans at commercial banks and credit unions.

Life Insurance Companies

Life insurance companies are a source of credit for certain policyholders who own life insurance policies that include a savings component, or cash value. Savings accumulate in a life insurance policy when scheduled payments, or premiums, exceed the cost of the death benefits that are being purchased by the policyholder. In general, life insurance policies with constant premiums include a savings feature, even though the premiums typically must be paid for many years before a cash value of significant size is available for borrowing. Term insurance, an inexpensive form of life insurance that provides a death benefit but no savings or cash value, cannot be used for loans by policyholders.

Life insurance loans often carry relatively low interest rates compared with the rates you would be charged on other types of consumer loans. The determination of the rate you will be required to pay to borrow funds from your life insurance policy will be specified in the policy. It is important to understand that life insurance loans involve borrowing your own money (i.e.,

> **Tip** Don't overlook your life insurance policy as a source of low-cost credit. You can often borrow more cheaply from your life insurance policy than from a financial institution. Also, life insurance loans have the advantage of not imposing a deadline for when the loan must be repaid.

you borrow savings that have accumulated in the policy), and that any loan outstanding at the time of your death will be deducted from the policy's death benefit. Still, borrowing from a life insurance policy that has accumulated a cash value is an alternative that should be considered when you are shopping for a loan.

Brokerage Firms

Brokerage firms serve as a source of credit when securities you own are being held in a margin account. The maximum you are permitted to borrow depends on the market value of the securities you own and the percentage of market value the brokerage firm will lend. Investors are generally permitted to borrow approximately 70 percent of the current market value of the securities being held. Although there is no specific date on which the loan must be repaid, additional collateral (more cash or securities) may be required if there is a decline in the market value of the securities in your account. Money that you borrow against securities you own may be used for any purpose, not just for investment needs. In other words, it may be to your advantage to borrow money from your brokerage account rather than arrange an installment loan when purchasing a new appliance.

Friends and Relatives

If you have been turned down for a loan by several banks and you consider the interest rate being charged by the local finance companies you have visited to be too high, you may decide that your only real alternative is to seek financial assistance from a relative or close friend. Perhaps you will be able to borrow at a favorable interest rate and still provide your relative or friend with a superior investment return. Sounds good, but on second thought, maybe it isn't so good.

Borrowing from a relative or friend may allow you to obtain favorable repayment terms, but this may come at the expense of damaging a personal relationship, especially if you find yourself unable to meet the terms of the loan or if you and the other individual have a misunderstanding concerning the terms of the loan. Personal loans from relatives or friends frequently have unclear terms that can be subject to different interpretations. You should also be aware that moving to a debtor-creditor association typically changes a relationship in which two people have been equals. Borrowing from a friend or relative may allow you to obtain a low interest rate, but potentially it has a high cost of another kind. Becoming a lender to a friend or relative entails the same dangers as becoming a borrower.

3 The Cost of Borrowing

Individuals sometimes spend weeks or months shopping for the best deal on an automobile or some other item and then squander most or all of their hard-earned savings by accepting whatever terms are offered to finance the purchase. Financing costs often comprise a substantial portion of the overall cost of ownership, so it is important to understand how financing costs are calculated and what actions you can take to reduce these costs.

Some Facts about Interest Rates

The interest rate you are required to pay to borrow money is influenced by many factors relating both to you and to the particular type of loan you choose. The length of time a loan is to be outstanding, the collateral (if any) that is pledged to the lender, your credit history, and the lender that is chosen are each important determinants of the interest rate you will be charged on a loan. Interest rates are also influenced by factors outside your control and unrelated to the specifics of your particular loan. No matter how much collateral you offer or how painstakingly you search among lenders for the most favorable terms on a loan, you will almost certainly be unable to finance your home at an interest rate of less than 3 percent. Likewise, you will be unable to obtain a 2 percent auto loan from a financial institution, or a 1 percent loan from your broker, no matter how excellent your credit history. I know, I know. You were able to obtain zero percent financing on a new car loan. But this was a giveaway to move vehicles off the lot at prices consumers would not ordinarily pay without some type of incentive.

The importance of outside influences on interest rates doesn't mean that the details of your particular loan don't count for much in determining the interest rate you pay. It does mean that conditions in the credit markets will play a major role in determining the terms of any loan you obtain. Unprecedented low levels of short-term interest rates made possible the zero-percent-interest vehicle loans and temporary offers from credit card issuers. In other words, the zero percent interest rate financing was an incentive that didn't really cost the lenders very much at the time it was offered.

The Importance of Economic Activity

Economic conditions have an important influence on interest rates. Interest rates tend to increase during periods of strong economic activity, when demand for credit is high. A vigorous

> **Tip**
>
> Rip-off artists often target consumers with credit problems or customers who have difficulty obtaining credit. One scam is to guarantee that applicants will obtain the credit they want in exchange for an up-front fee. It is likely you will kiss the fee you pay goodbye without gaining access to credit. Most legitimate lenders will not guarantee a loan before you apply, especially if you have a bad credit record.

economy causes businesses to borrow funds that can be used to expand their output of goods and services. At the same time, high employment and wage increases that accompany economic expansion are likely to put consumers in an optimistic mood, leading them to buy more goods and services on credit. Credit demand that accompanies a strong economy allows lenders to increase the interest rates they charge on loans; it also causes these lenders to have to offer higher returns to savers in order to attract the savers' money.

An economy mired in weakness does little to stimulate credit demand from businesses or consumers. Periods of weak economic activity are accompanied by idle manufacturing capacity, causing a decline in credit needs by most businesses, which are in no mood to expand. Likewise, rising unemployment that accompanies a weak economy causes consumers to become cautious and cut back on their spending and borrowing. The slack demand for credit during periods of weak economic activity tends to result in a decline in interest rates.

The Importance of Inflationary Expectations

Consumer, business, and government inflationary expectations have an important influence on the level of interest rates. Lenders that anticipate rising prices for goods and services will attempt to charge higher interest rates in order to seek compensation for the likelihood that loans will be repaid with devalued dollars. A lender that anticipates a 5 percent inflation rate is not inclined to willingly suffer a loss of purchasing power by making loans at an interest rate of 3 percent. Figure 7 illustrates the historical relationship between the consumer price index and interest rates as measured by the yield on ten-year U.S. Treasury securities. The major decline in inflation beginning in the mid-1970s was a pivotal factor in the decline in long-term

Figure 7 ■ Interest Rates and Inflation, 1965–2004

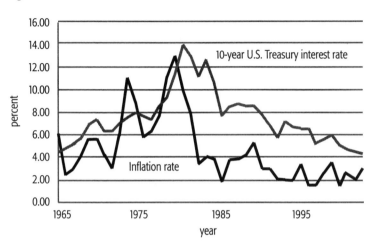

interest rates that commenced shortly thereafter. The decline in interest rates, in turn, was a key factor in the ensuing bull market in stocks.

At the same time that lenders view inflation as a reason to charge higher interest rates, potential borrowers, anticipating a high inflation rate, are likely to accept higher rates because they expect to be able to repay lenders with devalued dollars. Anticipated inflation of home values has proved to be a great incentive for individuals to borrow substantial sums of money in order to purchase expensive houses. Inflation is often accompanied by rising consumer income and business revenues, which make it easier for borrowers to repay their debt obligations. Anticipation of rising inflation also stimulates consumers and businesses to buy as soon as possible in order to beat expected price increases. Accelerated purchases by consumers and businesses increase the demand for credit, which, in turn, drives interest rates upward.

The Importance of Government Policy

Policies and actions of the federal government have a major impact on interest rates. Large federal deficits that result when federal expenditures exceed tax revenues require the government to borrow tens or hundreds of billions of dollars annually. Large amounts of government borrowing can cause great strains in the credit markets by siphoning funds away from businesses and consumers. Huge federal deficits during the late 1980s and early 1990s, and beginning again in 2003, caused the government to have to borrow hundreds of billions of dollars that could otherwise have been available to businesses and individuals. Much of this government borrowing was from lenders outside the United States. Large government deficits increase the demand for credit and exert upward pressure on interest rates.

The federal government continually intervenes in the credit markets to influence interest rates and guide the nation's economic activity. The Federal Reserve Board (frequently referred to as the "Fed"), an independent agency headed by presidential appointees, orchestrates government intervention in the economy and has a major impact on short-term interest rates. The Federal Reserve acts as a banker to commercial banks. It clears checks, makes loans, and establishes the amount of reserves that member banks must maintain against deposits. The Fed even establishes the proportion of a stock purchase that an investor is permitted to finance with borrowed money. The Federal Reserve has several tools at its disposal for influencing the credit markets.

- The Federal Reserve establishes the interest rate (called the *discount rate*) that commercial banks must pay when they borrow from the Fed. Commercial banks often borrow from the Fed when the banks need reserves or additional funds for making loans. A change in the discount rate is likely to cause commercial banks to change the interest rates they charge on loans to business and individual borrowers.

- The Fed is constantly buying and selling Treasury securities in the financial markets. These transactions (called *open-market operations*) have a major impact on the money supply, credit availability, and short-term interest rates. A substantial purchase of Treasury securities by the Federal Reserve causes new funds to flow into the banking system (cash replaces Treasury securities), which then has more funds available to lend. The availability of additional funds generally causes a decline in short-term interest rates. A large sale of Treasury securities by the Federal Reserve absorbs deposits and reserves from the banking system, thereby causing banks to increase interest rates and cut back on lending.

- Public announcements by a member of the Federal Reserve, especially the chairman, can have powerful effects on the credit markets. If a board member indicates that the Fed is concerned about a resumption of inflation, interest rates are likely to rise in anticipation of efforts by the Federal Reserve to tighten credit. The chairman of the Federal Reserve is considered one of the most powerful people in the country.

The Importance of Maturity Length

A loan's maturity length (i.e., the length of time before the loan is completely repaid) generally affects the rate of interest that will be charged on the loan. Loans with longer maturities typically entail higher interest rates, so you will generally be required to pay a higher rate of interest on a 30-year home mortgage than on a 15-year mortgage for the same amount of money for the same house. You are also likely to have to pay a

Figure 8 ■ **Interest Rates and Maturity Length (late 2004)**

	Length	Rate (%)
New auto loans	36 months	5.63
	48 months	5.89
	60 months	5.90
Home mortgages	15 years	4.81
	30 years	5.36
Certificates of deposit	6 months	1.75
	1 year	2.25
	2 years	2.85
	3 years	3.30
	5 years	3.90

higher interest rate on a 5-year car loan than on a 3-year car loan—not always, but usually. The direct relationship between the length of a loan and the interest rate charged is illustrated in Figure 8. Notice that the rate charged on car loans increases slightly with loans of longer maturities. Likewise, the rate on 30-year mortgages is higher than the rate charged on 15-year mortgages. An interest rate difference of a little less than one half of one percent can result in one's paying substantially more interest over many years on a large amount of money borrowed. The figure also shows that interest rates on certificates of deposit increase with an increase in maturity length. Observe the relationship between time and interest rates by checking the rates being offered on certificates of deposit the next time you visit your local bank or savings and loan association.

A loan with a long repayment period places the lender at greater risk than a loan requiring a short payback. A lender finds it much more difficult to evaluate a borrower's ability and willingness to repay a 30-year loan compared to a loan scheduled for repayment in six months. Even company officers with an intimate knowledge of their firm's operations will have less than total confidence in a 30-year forecast for their firm. The task of making judgments far into the future is that much tougher for lenders that have less familiarity with the firm.

Unanticipated inflation can cause major losses in purchasing power for lenders that make long-term loans. Imagine being in the position of a lender who loans money at a 6 percent interest rate for 20 years only to find several years after the loan is granted that annual inflation has increased to 9 percent annually. The funds that are due from the borrower will be deteriorating in value so rapidly that you will lose purchasing power during each year the loan is outstanding. Anticipated inflation is built into the terms of a loan (i.e., it is included in the interest rate), but unanticipated inflation can prove devastating to a lender, especially over a long period of time.

The positive relationship between Treasury maturities and interest rates does not always carry over to consumer and business loans. For example, loans with similar terms but different collateral are likely to have different interest rates. A one-year personal loan without collateral may have a higher interest rate than a three-year car loan, because the car pledged as collateral provides the lender with added security. Likewise, a six-month personal loan may carry a higher interest rate than a one-year personal loan, so as to allow the lender to recover expenses that are incurred in making the loan (e.g., employee time, paperwork, and credit research).

The Importance of Collateral

The potential for a borrower to default on a loan is one of the chief risks faced by a lender. Companies periodically encounter poor business conditions, and individuals occasionally become

> **Tip** You may be able to reduce interest expenses by consolidating your debt through a second mortgage or a home-equity line of credit. The problem is these loans require your home as collateral, meaning you could lose your home if you can't make the required payments. Another danger is that you may use the expanded credit availability to undertake even more spending.

unemployed. If a borrower encounters such circumstances, it is less likely that the borrower's outstanding debts will be fully repaid. A lender holding only a borrower's promise to repay stands to lose a substantial amount of money in the event the borrower is unable to meet the terms of the loan. Although a lender has legal avenues available to attempt to recover the principal of the loan, the borrower may owe several other lenders and possess few assets of any value.

A lender enjoys a more secure financial position when a borrower has pledged specific assets as collateral for a loan. In the event the borrower is unable to repay the loan, the lender can force the sale of the collateral and utilize funds from the sale to recover the unpaid interest and remaining balance on the loan. Collateral that improves a lender's financial position should result in a reduced interest rate to the borrower. The greater the

> **Tip** Make it a point to pay off your most expensive debt first. Generally this means keeping credit card balances as close to zero as possible. It doesn't make sense to pay ahead on a 5 percent home mortgage with tax-deductible interest at the same time you have outstanding credit card balances that are running up interest at a rate of 12 to 14 percent.

Figure 9 ■ Comparative Interest Rates of Different Types of Loans

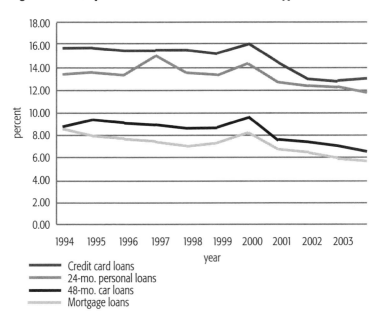

value of the collateral compared to the amount borrowed, the less the risk to the lender, and the more the interest rate on the loan should be reduced. Figure 9 illustrates the level of interest rates for different types of consumer-related loans during the past decade. Notice that credit card loans and personal loans, both of which are unsecured, typically have significantly higher interest rates than mortgages and car loans, both of which are secured by assets.

The Cost of Borrowing

Suppose you are offered a $5,000 loan to be repaid in six monthly installments of $900 each. Total repayment amounts to $5,400 (6 × $900), meaning that you will be charged interest of $400 ($5,400, the total amount of the payments, less $5,000, the amount you have borrowed). The lender claims the loan offers an attractive interest rate of $400/$5,000 (the amount of interest to be charged divided by the amount of money that is borrowed), or 8 percent. Is the interest rate of 8 percent quoted for this loan accurate, or is the lender attempting to hoodwink you?

Calculating Interest Rates

In the simplest type of loan, the interest rate is calculated as the dollar amount of interest you are charged divided by the amount of money borrowed. If you borrow $1,000 that must be repaid along with $60 in interest at the end of one year, you are being charged an interest rate of $60/$1,000, or 6 percent. The general formula for calculating the interest rate on a loan is:

$$i = I/P$$

where:
i is the interest rate
I is the dollar amount of interest paid
P is the amount borrowed

In real life most loans are more complicated than this example. Loans often involve a term of other than one year, and many loans are repaid with a series of payments rather than with a single payment. Some loans require periodic interest payments by the borrower until a predetermined date, at which time the initial amount borrowed becomes due. Because the specifics of individual loans can differ so much, it is worthwhile to familiarize yourself with some of the more important conventions and details that affect interest rates.

Interest rates are quoted on an annual basis. Certain financial variables, including inflation, investment returns, and interest rates, are nearly always computed and quoted on an annual, or yearly, basis. An adjustment is required to annualize the interest rate for loans with terms of other than one year. Suppose you borrow $1,000 and sign a loan agreement that requires you to repay $1,060 in 3 months. You are paying the same dollar interest required by the one-year loan agreement discussed on page 48, but now you have use of the borrowed money for only 3 months rather than a full year. The interest rate on this loan must be annualized to account for the shorter term. First, divide the number of months the loan is scheduled to be outstanding (in this case, 3 months) into the number of months in a year (always 12). The result (12 ÷ 3 = 4) is multiplied by the interest rate calculated from the previous formula. The annualized rate for the 3-month loan is ($60/$1,000) × (12 months/3 months), or 6 percent times 4, or 24 percent; the same amount borrowed, the same dollar amount of interest paid, for one-fourth the time, means four times the interest rate. If $60 in interest is charged for a $1,000 loan that is to be repaid in two years, the annualized interest rate would be ($60/$1,000) × (12 months/24 months), or 3 percent. You must always make certain that you and a lender are using the same assumptions in discussing the interest rate on a loan.

A loan's repayment schedule may have a significant impact on the interest rate you will pay. Suppose you borrow $3,000 for one year. At the end of the year, you are required to repay the $3,000 that has been borrowed plus $300 interest. This arrangement permits you to retain control of the entire amount borrowed ($3,000) for a full year, an agreement that results in a true 10 percent rate of interest. A requirement to pay interest or a portion of the principal prior to the loan's maturity creates an increase in a loan's effective rate of interest. Suppose an alternative loan agreement allows you to borrow the same $3,000, except that the principal and $300 interest are to be gradually paid over the one-year life of the loan. In this case 10 percent of the amount borrowed is added to the amount borrowed and the sum divided by 12, the number of months in a year. This

Figure 10 ■ Effective Interest Rates for Different Loan Payment Schedules

Suppose you approach several lenders with the same loan request to borrow $3,000 for one year. Each lender quotes an interest rate of 10%, but they all offer different repayment plans.

Lender One gives you $3,000 now and requires that you make a single payment of $3,300 at the end of one year.

Lender Two gives you $3,000 now and requires that you make 12 monthly payments of $263.75. Each payment takes care of the monthly interest charge and results in a slight reduction of the principal owed.

Lender Three gives you $3,000 now and requires 12 monthly payments of $275. The payments are determined by adding 10% in interest ($300) to the $3,000 you are borrowing and dividing the sum ($3,300) by 12.

Lender Four subtracts the 10% interest from $3,000 and gives you $2,700 now. Twelve monthly payments are established at $3,000 divided by 12, or $250.

Lender	Loan Amount Received	Payments	Total Payments	Effective Interest Rate
One	$3,000	$3,300	$3,300	10.00%
Two	3,000	263.75/mo	3,165	10.15%
Three	3,000	275.00/mo	3,300	18.46%
Four	2,700	250.00/mo	3,000	20.51%

second loan agreement requires 12 monthly payments of $275 each, or the same total of $3,300. A loan agreement in which the total amount of interest is added to the amount borrowed and the sum is divided by the number of payments to determine the size of each payment is known as the *add-on interest method,* and it results in a higher effective rate of interest. Figure 10 illustrates four different payment schedules for the $3,000 loan, each resulting in a different effective rate of interest.

Given the choice of paying $3,300 at the end of the year or $275 per month for one year, which should you choose? Or does it really matter? It is to your advantage to choose the single payment of $3,300, because you pay the same dollar amount of interest ($300) but have, on average, a larger amount of money borrowed. Add-on interest significantly increases the effective cost of a loan.

Interest collected on a loan's front end increases the effective interest rate. Certain installment loans, known as *discount loans,* are structured to allow the lender to collect the total amount of the interest at the time the loan is made. The effect of a discount loan is to charge interest on money that is not made available to the borrower. Suppose you borrow $3,000 for one year at a quoted rate of 10 percent. The lender deducts $300 in interest charges (10 percent × $3,000) and writes you a check for the balance of $2,700. The loan obligates you to pay 12 monthly installments of $250, or a total of $3,000. Quoting 10 percent interest for this loan is misleading. First, monthly payments require you to repay interest charges and a portion of the principal each month. Repaying principal throughout the term of the loan means you do not have the use of all the money that you have borrowed for the full term. Second, interest is being charged on $3,000 even though you actually receive only $2,700 from the lender. Discounted interest increases the effective interest rate by requiring you to pay interest on more money than you receive.

Interest can be calculated on a simple or a compounded basis. Suppose you are interested in obtaining a $3,000 loan. One bank offers the loan at a 10 percent annual interest rate with principal of $3,000 and interest of $300 (10 percent × $3,000) to be paid at the end of one year. Interest calculated only on the original principal of a loan is known as simple interest. Simple interest on the same loan for two years would be $600, or twice the interest for one year. A second bank offers a loan at the same stated rate of 10 percent but requires that you pay $25 (one month's interest, or one-twelfth of $300) at the end of each of 12 months. The last interest payment is to be accompanied by repayment of the $3,000 principal. Paying interest monthly, or, alternatively, having the lender calculate interest in each subsequent month on both principal and accumulated interest is known as compounding. Compounding increases the effective rate of interest earned by savers (e.g., a savings account that pays interest quarterly or semiannually rather than annually) and increases the cost of borrowed money.

Creditors sometimes use different loan balances to calculate finance charges. It has already been pointed out that creditors sometimes calculate finance charges on the full amount borrowed even though installment payments will gradually reduce the balance that is owed over the life of the loan. Credit card companies also utilize several methods to calculate finance charges to cardholders. Some issuers credit any payments that have been made before calculating your finance charges. It is to your advantage to receive credit for payments you have made, because the credit reduces the loan balance on which interest is calculated. Other credit card issuers calculate finance charges for a specific period, without taking account of payments that have been

> **Tip**
>
> Creditors are permitted to charge a late fee in the event you do not make your loan payment on time. However, creditors cannot charge late fees simply because you have not paid a late fee you already owe. This means that if you do not include the late fee you owe with your next regular payment, the creditor cannot subtract the late fee from your payment and then charge you a second late fee because the current payment is insufficient.

made during the period. This latter method works to your disadvantage, because a higher loan balance is used to calculate the finance charges. Still other credit card issuers calculate a finance charge that is based on the average daily balance of your borrowing. All these different methods of calculating finance charges on credit card balances are discussed more fully in Chapter 6. Suffice it to say that the finance charge you are assessed on a credit card balance depends to a large degree on the calculation method utilized by the issuer. The method of calculating a finance charge is of little consequence if you regularly pay off your credit card balance in full each month.

Purchasing credit insurance increases the cost of a loan. Many lenders attempt to convince borrowers to purchase credit insurance that ensures repayment of a loan in the event the borrower dies, becomes disabled, or suffers a loss of property. The premium cost of the insurance is added to the amount being financed, so a borrower ends up paying interest on this additional expense. Credit insurance is a profitable financial product that is aggressively sold by many lenders, and such insurance is sometimes required to gain approval for a loan. Credit insurance also benefits lenders, in that they don't have to be concerned about how a loan will be repaid in the event the borrower dies or becomes

Tip Credit insurance that is designed to repay the balance of a loan in the event of the death of the borrower is generally a bad buy. Think carefully before accepting credit insurance that is offered by a lender.

disabled. Many financial advisers suggest that credit insurance is a luxury most borrowers should decline.

The Annual Percentage Rate: A Comparable Measure of Interest

Because several different calculations can be used to come up with an interest rate quotation, it is fortunate that there is an accepted standard for computing the cost of borrowing money. A standardized calculation allows you to compare the interest rates being offered by different lenders. Without a standardized method of calculation, it is difficult to know for certain whether the lowest quoted rate is, in fact, the lowest actual rate.

The standard measure of the cost of borrowing is known as the annual percentage rate (APR). Knowing the APR is useful regardless of whether you are in the market for an installment loan or a single-payment loan. The Consumer Credit Protection Act of 1968 (also called the Truth in Lending Law) requires that all creditors, including banks, savings and loan associations, car dealers, retailers, finance companies, and credit card companies, provide a borrower with a loan's total finance charges and APR. These two pieces of information allow you to compare the offerings of various lenders. Remember, interest rates are comparable only when they have been calculated in the same manner.

Now it is time to review the question posed earlier in this chapter. To refresh your memory, you are being offered a $5,000 loan that requires six monthly payments of $900 each.

Figure 11 ■ Calculating the Annual Percentage Rate (APR) for a Loan

A loan's annual percentage rate can be closely approximated using the following formula:

$$i = \frac{2 \times n \times I}{P(N + 1)}$$

where:

i is the annual percentage rate

n is the number of payment periods in one year

I is the total financing charges (mostly interest)

P is the principal (the amount borrowed)

N is the number of scheduled payments

Suppose you borrow $10,000 to purchase a used VW camper, and the loan is to be repaid in 24 monthly payments of $500 each. Each payment covers monthly interest plus a portion of the outstanding balance on the loan. The total payments required by the loan agreement amount to 24 × $500, or $12,000. The loan's total cost of credit equals the total of your payments ($12,000) less the amount you borrow ($10,000), or $2,000. The APR on the loan is calculated as follows:

$$\frac{2 \times 12 \times \$2,000}{\$10,000 (24 + 1)} = \frac{\$48,000}{\$250,000} = 19.2\%$$

The lender tells you that you will be paying 8 percent interest, as calculated by dividing the total interest charge ($5,400 less $5,000, or $400) by the amount borrowed ($5,000). One problem is that the lender is requiring you to repay the loan in installments but quoting an interest rate based on your having the full amount of the loan available for the entire six months. Also, the lender has failed to annualize the rate to adjust for the scheduled payoff in six months, not one year.

Using the APR formula presented in Figure 11, the interest rate on this loan is calculated as

$$i = \frac{2 \times 12 \times \$400}{\$5,000(6 + 1)} = \frac{\$9,600}{\$35,000} = 27.4\%$$

This calculation presents quite a different picture of the relative cost of the loan compared with the 8 percent rate that has been quoted by the lender.

Early Repayment of a Loan

Perhaps you have received a fat raise or inherited money from your deceased aunt's estate and decide to repay a loan before its scheduled due date. The early repayment should reduce your total financing costs because the lender's money will be returned ahead of schedule. On the other hand, will you be required to compensate the lender, who stands to lose interest income because of your early repayment?

Potential penalties and rebates in financing costs caused by a loan's early repayment should be addressed in the contract that is signed at the time the loan is finalized. Some agreements permit a borrower to prepay a loan without penalty. Suppose you borrow $5,000 for one year, with interest and principal to be

> **Tip**
>
> If you are a good money manager who prefers to take care of things ahead of time, try to avoid having prepayment penalties included in a loan contract. You don't want to incur a penalty in the event you have extra funds that can be used to pay down the balance on a loan and reduce future interest expense. Ask about any prepayment penalty at the time the loan is negotiated.

Figure 12 ■ Calculating an Early Loan Payoff Using the Rule of 78s

Suppose you borrow $10,000 and sign a loan agreement that calls for 24 monthly payments of $500 each. The finance charges over the life of the loan equal the total of your scheduled payments ($12,000) less the amount you borrow ($10,000), or $2,000. After a year and a half (18 months), you decide that the extra cash in a savings account is paying such a paltry return that you may as well withdraw the savings and pay off the balance of the loan.

According to the rule of 78s, the lender will calculate your required payment by determining the sum of the digits for all the scheduled payments (i.e., 24 + 23 + 22 + . . . + 1, or 300) and the sum of the digits for the remaining payments (i.e., 6 + 5 + 4 + 3 + 2 + 1, or 21). The fraction determined by dividing the sum of the digits for the remaining payments (21) by the sum of the digits of the entire loan (300) is multiplied by the total finance charge ($2,000) to determine the scheduled interest you should not have to pay since the loan will be paid off early. This reduction in interest is subtracted from the sum of all the remaining payments to determine the amount you will be required to pay in order to retire the debt after 18 months.

The fraction of total interest that should be forgiven because of early repayment is as follows:

$$\frac{\text{sum of the digits of remaining payments}}{\text{sum of the digits of all payments}} = \frac{21}{300} = 0.070$$

The scheduled interest included in the last 6 payments that should be forgiven is equal to the fraction calculated above times the total financing charge, or

$$0.070 \times \$2,000 = \$140$$

The amount required to pay off the loan early is equal to the sum of the remaining payments less the amount of interest that is included in the payments, or

$$(6 \times \$500) - \$140 = \$2,860$$

repaid in one single, end-of-year payment. If you decide to repay the loan at the end of six months and are not charged a penalty, you will be charged only half the scheduled finance charges.

The Rule of 78s

The amount required for early repayment of an installment loan is more difficult to compute than that for a single-payment loan, because installment loans involve series of equal payments that are allocated partly to interest and partly to principal reduction. When an installment loan is to be repaid early, the lender must determine how much of the remaining payments represent financing charges to be deducted in calculating the payoff. If you intend to pay off a loan that has 15 remaining payments of $400 each, you should not be required to repay 15 times $400, or $6,000, because these payments include interest that should not be charged.

Lenders frequently use the rule of 78s to determine the amount that must be paid by a borrower who wishes to repay an installment loan ahead of schedule. (The 78 stands for the sum of the digits 1–12, the number of months in a one-year loan.) The rule of 78s provides a method to calculate the amount of interest that is embodied in all the remaining installment payments. For example, if you are scheduled to make an additional 12 monthly payments of $400 each, and the rule of 78s determines that interest of $500 is included in these payments, you will be required to come up with 12 × $400, or $4,800, less $500, or $4,300. Figure 12 illustrates the calculation used to determine the early payoff on a loan using the rule of 78s.

4 Obtaining a Loan

Knowing how and where to search for a lender and how best to apply for a loan increases the likelihood that you will be successful in obtaining the money you seek on the best possible terms. Chapter 2 identified various categories of lenders and their respective lending specialties. This information will help you to concentrate your search among creditors that are most likely to be offering the type of loan you are seeking. Don't waste both your time and a lender's time by wandering from one financial institution to another without regard to the kinds of loans the firms generally make.

Determining What Is Important

Once you have identified several likely sources of money, determine the most effective way to approach each of these prospects. Begin by imagining yourself on the opposite side of the lending desk. If you were the lender, what considerations would be important in deciding whether to approve the loan request? What kinds of information would you ask for? You would surely want to know if the applicant has other loans outstanding, including the balances and required payments on the loans. The amount, sources, and stability of the applicant's income would help you assess the applicant's ability to meet current debts plus the added burden of an additional loan. A modest income combined with relatively heavy existing debt payments typically signals trouble and casts doubt on the applicant's ability to handle even more debt. You are likely to want a record of the applicant's job history, on the theory that employment stability increases the likelihood that the terms of a loan agreement will be honored. The types of information you would request from a loan applicant are probably very similar to what a lender will request from you.

The U.S. Federal Trade Commission (FTC) is charged with enforcing several federal credit laws that are likely to apply to the lenders and to the loan you seek. For example, creditors are prohibited from discriminating because of sex, marital status, and several other factors. In other words, it shouldn't matter if you are a female or a member of a minority. Likewise, there are established standards that provide borrowers with information on the cost of credit and terms of repayment. Figure 13 provides a summary of six major federal credit laws administered by the FTC.

Identifying the Loan You Prefer

Shopping for a loan is in many ways similar to shopping for a washing machine, an automobile, a new home, or a frozen pizza. You set out to locate a particular good or service that best satisfies your needs at the lowest possible cost. Loans, like most goods and services, are offered in several forms, from the most basic to the very fancy, and at widely varying prices. Just as you must determine which make and model of washing machine best satisfies your laundry needs (size, color, electronic vs. manual controls, etc.), so too should you identify the type of loan

Figure 13 ■ A Summary of Federal Credit Laws

The Equal Credit Opportunity Act Prohibits credit discrimination because of sex, race, marital status, religion, national origin, or age, or because the applicant receives public assistance.

Consumer Credit Reporting Reform Act Establishes standards for credit bureau reports and specifies who can obtain access to the reports. Allows a consumer to review his or her credit file and correct inaccuracies. Sets rules for settling disputes between consumers and credit-reporting agencies.

The Fair Credit Billing Act Establishes standards for providing billing information and settling disputes between creditors and debtors. Allows a merchant to give cash discounts to customers who pay cash rather than use credit.

Fair Debt Collection Practices Act Prohibits debt collectors from using unfair and deceptive practices to collect overdue bills that a creditor has forwarded for collection.

Fair Credit and Charge Card Disclosure Act Establishes standards of disclosure for issuers of credit cards.

Truth in Lending Act Requires that lenders provide borrowers with written disclosures of the cost of credit and the terms of repayment before borrowers enter into credit transactions. Prohibits issuers from sending credit cards to individuals who do not request them. Establishes maximum liability for lost or stolen credit cards.

The FTC is charged with enforcing federal credit laws. Additional information on these laws can be obtained by writing: Public Reference, Federal Trade Commission, Washington, DC 20580. Information is also available at the FTC website at http://www.ftc.gov.

---

that best meets your particular borrowing requirements. Some of the basic decisions you should come to grips with before seeking a lender include the following:

How much you wish to borrow The first thing you need to determine is the amount of money you need. This requires that you estimate the cost of whatever it is you intend to buy or do. What is the cost of the new car, the summer-long vacation, private school tuition, your dream home, or the payoff on your credit card account? Can you imagine sitting across from a potential borrower and asking, "How much money do you want to borrow?" and having the borrower, with a puzzled look, scratch his head and reply, "Gee, I'm pretty flexible on that." Impressive, huh?

The length of time the money will be needed Do you need the money for a month, six months, a year, or 20 years? Perhaps you need $2,500 to pay college tuition and expect to be able to repay a loan within a month, when financial aid approval is expected. If the aid isn't forthcoming, you feel that you should be able to pay off the loan and finance charges by the end of one year. On the other hand, perhaps you are planning to purchase a new home and require a loan of 20 or more years. Your ability to make the required payments will be a major factor in determining an appropriate maturity. The more income you will have available to meet loan payments, the shorter the maturity of a loan you can handle, and the less total interest you will pay.

Your preferred method of repayment Would you prefer to retire the loan with a series of equal monthly payments, or would you rather repay the entire amount of the loan in one lump sum? If you choose the single-payment option, would you prefer to pay interest charges annually, or would you rather have interest charges accumulate until the date on which the loan is scheduled for repayment? It is generally wise to build some flexibility into your repayment preference, because it may appear unreal-

Figure 14 ■ What Creditors Cannot Do

When you apply for credit, a creditor cannot:
- ask whether you are divorced or widowed.
- ask about your plans for having or raising children.
- discourage you from applying because of your sex, marital status, age, or national origin, or because you receive public assistance income.
- ask about your marital status if you are applying for a separate, unsecured account and you do not live in a community property state.
- ask for information about your spouse, unless the spouse will have access to the account or you will be relying on your spouse's income to support your application.
- consider your age, except when you are underage or when the creditor favors you because of your age.

When deciding to give you credit, a creditor cannot:
- consider your sex, marital status, race, national origin, or religion.
- consider the race of the people who live in the neighborhood where you want to buy or improve a house with borrowed money.
- refuse to consider income from public assistance, part-time employment, pensions, or consistently received alimony or child support payments.

---

istic in the eyes of the potential lenders. For example, you can expect to encounter difficulty locating a lender that makes a single-payment car loan.

The Things Lenders Consider Important

As previously mentioned, lenders are primarily interested in whether a potential borrower is likely to fulfill the requirements of a loan agreement. A lender will be more disposed to act favorably on your loan application if you are viewed as someone who will make a full and timely repayment. Remember, a creditor lends you money in the expectation of earning a profit—an unlikely outcome if there is a good possibility that you will default on your loan. It is also important to know that lenders are required by federal law to follow certain guidelines in their dealings with you. Figure 14 provides a listing of things that creditors cannot do when you apply for credit.

Lenders vary in the methods they employ for evaluating loan applicants. Indeed, a single lender may use different methods to evaluate different applicants. Some lenders may emphasize personal qualities as evidenced from a personal interview and contacts with references. Other lenders strictly follow a list of established guidelines related to income, length of employment, current debts and loan payments, family size, and so forth. Many lenders take an intermediate approach and judge a loan applicant on the basis of both subjective and objective measures.

Figure 15 ■ Building a Good Credit Record

It is often difficult to obtain credit on your first attempt. Most creditors will want to examine your credit record in addition to looking at information about your salary and employment. If you have no prior credit history, here are some methods to begin building one.

- Open a checking account, savings account, or both. Having accounts in your own name provides some evidence that you know how to manage money.

- Apply for a department store charge card. These are generally easier to obtain than national cards such as Visa and MasterCard, but their use allows you to build a credit record.

- Ask someone to cosign your credit application. Having a cosigner will allow you to use someone else's credit history to build your own credit history.

- Ask if a financial institution will issue you a credit card using your savings account as collateral. This arrangement will keep you from having full access to your savings until you qualify for credit without collateral.

- If you are turned down for credit, find out why and attempt to clear up any mistakes.

> **Tip**
>
> You are entering the financial trouble zone when you find yourself borrowing in order to be able to make payments on an existing loan. You have become overextended when you have difficulty making loan payments out of your current income.

Figure 15 offers some suggestions for actions you can take to help build a good credit record in order to make it easier to obtain loans at a favorable interest rate.

Character

From a lender's standpoint, character reflects the importance a potential borrower attaches to meeting his or her obligations, especially those of a financial nature. Any lender would hope to attract borrowers who will make every effort to repay their loans. A lender may make a character judgment primarily on subjective factors, such as your appearance and personal manner at the time you apply for a loan. A lender may also place a great deal of importance on the comments of references you are able to supply. Lenders are likely to put great stock in the opinion of other lenders with whom you have had previous dealings.

Character is also judged by more objective criteria. The extent to which you have fulfilled previous loan commitments is likely to be a key consideration when a lender evaluates your character. A series of previous loan defaults will almost certainly be viewed as a serious character flaw. The better able you are to convince a potential lender that you are a person who cares about your obligations and that you can be trusted with someone else's money, the more likely the character issue will be decided in your favor.

Capacity for Repayment

The amount of cash flow you have available to help meet the terms of a loan is a significant consideration for any creditor. The larger your income relative to your expenses and existing loan payments, the greater your capacity to make the required payments on an additional loan. Substantial capacity exists to make the payments on a new loan if you have considerable income, modest expenses, and few loan obligations. The stability of your income and the security of your employment are both important considerations for a lender, especially when you are requesting money for a relatively long period. In general, the more stable your income, in terms of both the amount and the source, the greater your capacity to meet a debt obligation.

Collateral

The collateral you are able to pledge on a loan helps ensure a lender against loss in the event you are unable to make the required payments. Sufficient collateral can often overcome other deficiencies in your loan application. Even if your character is suspect and your income is barely adequate relative to the size of the loan you are seeking, pledging substantial assets as collateral can help assure a lender that no money will be lost on a loan. The greater the value and liquidity of the assets you are able to pledge as collateral (liquid assets, by definition, are those that can easily be sold at fair market value), the more likely your loan application is to be approved.

Financial Assets You Own

The more financial assets you own free and clear of debt (i.e., assets that are not pledged as collateral against other loans), the greater a lender's confidence that you will be able to honor the

> **Tip**
>
> Arrange for financing ahead of the time you actually need the money. Having a lender's commitment allows you to shop for the best deal on whatever it is you are intending to purchase. Being in a hurry to obtain a loan because you need the money right away is likely to cause you to accept whatever loan terms a lender offers.

terms of a loan. Suppose you are interested in purchasing a new automobile. You have substantial investments in certificates of deposit, common stocks, and bonds that could be sold to raise the funds you need, but there may be reasons you would rather retain the financial assets and seek temporary funds from a lender. For example, there may be penalties or taxes you would have to pay on a sale of these investments. A lender is likely to view your assets as a reservoir that you can tap in the event you encounter a problem repaying your loan from regular income or cash flow.

The Importance of Your Credit File

Individual credit histories are of interest to enough parties that entrepreneurs have formed companies to collect and distribute information about individual credit dealings. Privately operated credit bureaus collect and maintain personal and credit information about millions of individuals, probably including yourself. Each month thousands of bureaus collect, record, and transmit information to one or more of the country's three major credit bureaus.

Your credit file that is maintained at one or more credit bureaus contains personal information including your name,

> **Tip** A creditor is not required to change a joint account to an individual account following a divorce. If the change is made, the creditor can require you to reapply for credit and, based on your new application, extend or deny you credit. Altering a mortgage or home-equity loan is likely to require refinancing to remove a spouse from the obligation.

current and former addresses, spouse, Social Security number, date of birth, current and past employers, and whether you rent or own your residence. The credit file also has financial information, including your income, a record of checks that have been returned for insufficient funds, and details of your past credit dealings. The credit record is likely to include the lending institution, loan amount, payment terms, and repayment history for each of your current and past loans. Credit files also contain legal information (e.g., bankruptcies and judgments) such as appears in public notices.

Credit bureaus are actually nothing more than clearinghouses that collect and share credit information among creditors and other interested parties. Credit bureaus don't make a decision on your loan application, rather they supply information to their members, who make their own judgments. Lenders are at once both the primary users of credit bureau information and

> **Tip** Always apply for credit using exactly the same name. For example, if you normally include your middle initial, always include your middle initial. Using the same name will result in more accurate reporting of your credit history in credit bureau files.

the suppliers of most of the data contained in credit bureau files. Creditors utilize credit bureaus to check on the accuracy of information provided by loan applicants (are you really employed by Monty Howell's Auto Equipment Suppliers?) and to determine if applicants have honored current and past credit agreements. Employers who wish to check on an applicant's former employment also find credit bureaus to be a valuable source of information.

Errors in Your Credit Report

Erroneous negative information that is part of your credit report can create major roadblocks to gaining credit or employment. There is ample opportunity for errors to creep into any system that involves daily postings and transfers of millions of pieces of information among millions of accounts. Credit data are sometimes posted to the wrong account, most frequently the account of someone who has an identical or similar name. Errors can occur when you use slightly different names (e.g., sometimes with your middle initial, sometimes without) to apply for credit.

In a credit file, personal information such as income and employment is often outdated, because it is typically entered only at the time you apply for credit, which may have last occurred several years ago. Confusion about some past transaction or credit relationship may cause faulty information to be part of your file. Perhaps a dispute with a creditor was eventually resolved, but the outcome escaped being posted in your account. An inquiry into the accuracy of credit information by a national consumer group found that nearly 20 percent of more than 150 credit files contained at least one error that was judged serious enough that it could result in denial of credit.

> **Tip** A joint credit application can come back to haunt former spouses following a divorce. A joint loan means that each is responsible for the debt, even if a divorce decree assigns separate debt obligations to each spouse. Former spouses who run up bills they don't pay can hurt their ex-partner's credit histories on jointly held accounts.

Correcting Errors in Your Credit File

Incorrect information in your credit file can cause you big headaches. Of course, correct information that puts you in a bad light can also cause difficulties. Most negative information remains in your file for seven years, and bankruptcy information may be retained for ten years. Without intervention on your part, incorrect negative information in your credit file spells long-term trouble for your dealings with potential employers and lenders.

Financial experts recommend that every three or four years, and at least six months prior to applying for a major loan, you should examine the information in your credit files at all three of the national credit reporting agencies noted in Figure 16. Allow adequate time to discover and clear up any errors. The clearing-up part can sometimes require more time than you

Figure 16 ■ The Three Major Credit Reporting Agencies

Equifax	**Experian**	**TransUnion**
P.O. Box 740241	P.O. Box 2002	P.O. Box 1000
Atlanta, GA 30374	Allen, TX 75013	Chester, PA 19022
1-800-685-1111	1-888-397-3742	1-800-916-8800
www.equifax.com	www.experian.com	www.transunion.com

expect. When sending for a copy of your credit file, request a brochure that outlines your legal rights with respect to the actions you may take.

You have a legal right to know what is in your credit file, although you may have to pay a small fee to obtain a copy of the contents. Equifax permits an individual to obtain one free copy of his or her credit file per calendar year. You have a right to view the contents of your credit file without charge in the event you have been denied credit because of information contained in the file. To obtain the free copy, you must initiate a request within 30 days of being denied credit. Contact the credit bureaus by using the information in Figure 16.

In the event you discover information in your file that you wish to dispute or have purged, what action should you take? First, you should complete and return the form that will be enclosed with your file, and include any supporting documentation you may have. For example, you may have a statement from a creditor indicating that you have successfully repaid a loan, whereas your credit report indicates that payments on the loan are behind schedule. If your credit file mistakenly contains information concerning someone else's financial dealings, you should contact both the credit bureau and the lender. The lender should have the borrower's Social Security number on file. Be certain to explain your side of the dispute clearly and concisely. Credit bureaus are required to undertake an investigation when they receive claims that their information is inaccurate or incomplete.

You have the right to include in your credit file a letter of up to 100 words explaining your side of the dispute. You may also find it useful to include a personal letter that addresses a negative item that is not in dispute. For example, you might want your file to include a note explaining why you fell behind on

Figure 17 ■ Sample Dispute Letter

The Federal Trade Commission recommends following this sample dispute letter in the event you find an error or misleading item in your credit report.

<u>Date</u>

<u>Your Name</u>
<u>Your Address</u>
<u>Your City, State, Zip Code</u>

<u>Complaint Department</u>
<u>Name of Credit Reporting Agency</u>
<u>Address</u>
<u>City, State, Zip Code</u>

Dear Sir or Madam:

I am writing to dispute the following information in my file. The items I dispute are also encircled on the attached copy of the report I received. (<u>Identify item or items disputed by name of source, such as creditors or tax court, and identify type of item, such as credit account, judgment, etc.</u>)

This item is (<u>inaccurate or incomplete</u>) because (<u>describe what is inaccurate or incomplete and why</u>). I am requesting that the item be deleted (<u>or request another specific change</u>) to correct the information.

Enclosed are copies of (<u>use this sentence if applicable and describe any enclosed documentation, such as payment records, court documents</u>) supporting my position. Please investigate this (<u>these</u>) matter(s) and (<u>delete or correct</u>) the disputed item(s) as soon as possible.

Sincerely,
<u>Your name</u>

<u>Enclosures: (list what you are enclosing)</u>

repaying a loan (e.g., you were in the hospital, caring for your sick parents, or out of work). In the event you are unable to reach an acceptable resolution of your dispute, appeal directly to the creditor or other source of the negative information to provide a letter or some other written material that supports your side of the disagreement. Figure 17 illustrates a sample dispute letter.

Credit Scoring

Although the information contained in your credit file is important, it is the lender, not the credit bureau, that will approve or disapprove your application for a loan. Lenders often reach decisions on credit applications by utilizing a grading system that evaluates information contained in credit bureau reports in addition to information provided on loan applications. A loan applicant receives assigned points based on various factors such as the length of time spent at the same address, age, length of tenure in the same job, amount of annual income, and number of dependents. High scores identify applicants who are expected to be good credit risks and who will be automatically approved for credit. Applicants with scores that fall in a medium range may require further evaluation or may be approved for a nominal amount of credit. A low score will generally doom an applicant, who must then search for another lender.

The components included in credit scoring systems and the relative importance of each component vary from lender to lender, depending on what factors a particular lender feels are critical in identifying good credit risks. The relative importance of individual factors such as job longevity and age are judged according to how accurately the factors have tracked past loan repayment performance. One lender may consider age to be

Figure 18 ■ Factors That Are Likely to Affect Your Credit Score

Although credit-scoring models are complex and tend to vary among creditors and different types of credit, most models evaluate the following types of information in your credit report:

- **Have you paid your bills on time?** Late payments, accounts referred to collection agencies, and bankruptcy will reduce your credit score.

- **What is your outstanding debt?** A high level of outstanding debt relative to your credit limits is likely to have a negative impact on your credit score.

- **How long is your credit history?** A short credit history is likely to reduce your credit score.

- **Have you recently applied for new credit?** Too many inquiries on your credit report will negatively impact your credit score.

- **How many and what types of credit accounts do you have?** Too many credit accounts of any type and accounts at finance companies are both likely to negatively affect your credit score.

---

only marginally useful in determining whether a borrower will successfully repay a loan, while another lender's experience may rate age to be an essential factor. Somewhat surprisingly, lenders are often more willing to grant credit when you already have access to substantial amounts of credit through holding several credit cards. Figure 18 provides a list of factors that credit reporting agencies are likely to consider in establishing your credit score.

Things to Take Care of Before You Apply for Credit

Several actions can be taken to improve your chances of success in obtaining a loan. Remember, it is to your advantage to make yourself as attractive a loan applicant as possible. Your goal is to convince a lender that you will successfully repay the loan you are seeking.

1. *Review your credit file.* The importance of this action cannot be overstressed. If your credit file contains negative information that is incorrect, you need to take action to have this information removed or corrected. If your file contains negative information that is not in dispute (i.e., you actually did mess up), provide a written explanation and request that it be included in your file. You have a legal right to do this.

2. *Prepare personal financial statements.* By now you should know that lenders will consider your loan request only after they have reviewed information concerning your income, outstanding debts, and credit history. Some of the information will be obtained from your credit report. It will be to your advantage to assemble this information, along with estimates of your income, expenses, assets, and liabilities, so that you can present it to potential lenders at the time you apply for a loan. The task of assembling this financial information allows you to update your own knowledge of your financial status before meeting with a lender. This information will allow you to better support your loan application. The financial statements, even though they may be rudimentary, combined with your own financial awareness, are likely to impress a lender and give you some leverage to bargain for

Tip Financial advisers generally counsel against applying for credit at several sources within a short period of time. Each creditor is likely to access your credit report and cause an inquiry to be recorded in your credit file. A large number of inquiries may raise a red flag and cause potential lenders to wonder if you are on a borrowing binge.

better terms (e.g., a lower interest rate and/or a more favorable repayment schedule).

At the least, you should determine your current income and rough out an estimate of your major expenses (rent or mortgage payment, auto loan payment, utilities, insurance premiums, etc.). Also, put together a list of your major assets (car, home, furniture, etc.) along with a listing of the balances and required payments on each of your outstanding loans. This is information any reputable creditor will eventually want to see, and you may as well become familiar with it before meeting with a lender. Understanding your financial condition will help you answer questions that may arise when you talk with a loan officer.

5 Managing Your Credit

Intelligent credit management will lead to a more enjoyable life, eventually. You will spend money more wisely, maintain control of your borrowing, save on the amount of interest you pay to creditors, and fall asleep without worrying about how you are going to make next week's loan payment. If this sounds like the result of some magic potion, don't be fooled. The benefits of intelligent credit management require a certain amount of sacrifice. You may find it necessary to eliminate, reduce, or delay some purchases you would like to make, because a credit management program places limitations on your borrowing. The major sacrifice of a credit management program is that of the purchases you may have to forgo, at least in the short run. Fortunately, in the long run, you should be able to acquire more of the things you really want, and generally at a lower overall cost.

Determining Your Debt Limit

Ability to handle debt is primarily a function of the income that is available to make the required payments to lenders. The income available for satisfying lenders is that portion that remains after you have met other required and basic spending

> **Tip** View credit as a necessary evil and borrow only as much as you need. Just because a creditor will lend 90 percent of the purchase price of a new vehicle or a home doesn't necessarily mean you should borrow this much. Using funds you have available to make a larger down payment can result in substantial interest savings.

needs, including taxes, insurance premiums, contributions to retirement, food, shelter, and clothing. Although considerable flexibility can exist for the amounts you spend in each of these categories (other than taxes), there is a limit to how much this spending can be reduced. The greater the amount of current and projected income that remains after your required spending is taken care of, the larger the debt payments you should be able to handle without becoming financially strapped. Being able to handle larger debt payments means you can safely borrow additional money. Figure 19 provides a historical guide of the household debt-service burden as a percent of disposable income (more commonly called *take-home pay*). Some financial analysts believe families are overextended when their debt payments total over 20 percent of disposable income.

Required spending needs depend on many factors that, in combination, are unique to your particular situation. Even something as basic as the state in which you reside plays a role in determining your spending requirements because of differences in living costs and differences in taxes levied by the various states. Even more important are your family situation and lifestyle. Compared to a family with several children, an individual spends considerably less money for most basic consumption items (other than sports cars). Thus, an individual who is free of family obligations is generally able to support substantially more debt than a family that earns the same income.

Figure 19 ■ **Household Debt-Service Burden as a Percentage of Disposable Income**

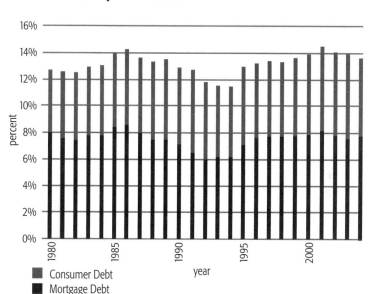

Consumer Debt
Mortgage Debt

year

Perhaps a simple example will serve to illustrate the relationship between income, required spending, and capacity to handle debt. Suppose you are considering a $3,000 loan to help pay for the restoration of a classic automobile (read that as "money pit") you recently purchased. You would like to borrow the money now so that you can begin work on the car; however, you don't want to take on a loan that will strap you financially. Your current take-home pay is $2,500 per month (i.e., after taxes, Social Security, health insurance, and your retirement contribution have been deducted from your gross income). You estimate that you spend approximately $1,700 each month for rent, utilities, food, insurance (other than health insurance that has already been considered), and clothing, which leaves $800 to

Figure 20 ■ Signs of Too Much Debt

- You pay only the minimum required payment on your credit cards.
- You borrow to make the required payments on your existing debt.
- You are missing payments to your creditors.
- The balances on your credit cards are increasing each month.
- You have little to no savings.
- Payments to creditors take such a large proportion of your income that little is left for necessities.
- You have to find extra work in order to meet your bills.
- You have gotten into the habit of raiding your savings in order to meet your monthly expenses.
- You don't expect to be able to repay your creditors.

support debt payments and other spending needs. This amount should prove adequate to service the payments on a $3,000 loan, even if repayment is to be made within one or two years. A two-year loan at 9 percent annual interest would require 24 monthly payments of $137 each. On the other hand, if your take-home pay is regularly depleted by the end of each month, you are in poor shape to take on a debt obligation unless you have the willingness and financial discipline to reduce your other spending. Figure 20 lists some of the warnings signs that you may have taken on too much debt.

The Importance of Maintaining a Personal Budget

Most individuals and families can derive substantial benefits from maintaining a personal budgeting system. The less money you have remaining at the end of any month and the more you wonder where your income has gone, the more you will benefit from a personal budget. From the standpoint of credit management, a budget allows you to determine your credit needs and to evaluate your ability to handle the required payments that credit entails. The financial planning required to maintain a budget makes it less likely that you will fall into the trap of borrowing to satisfy your immediate needs without first considering how this will affect your ability to take care of future needs. Keep in mind that most loans represent borrowing from future consumption in order to satisfy present needs. Financial planning is the key to controlling this borrowing with good credit management.

One of the steps to intelligent financial planning is developing a personal budget. Setting up a personal budget requires that you forecast your expected income and expenditures for the length of the budgeting period (e.g., six months, one year, two years, five years, or however long you decide is necessary). The forecast periods in a personal budget are typically set at the same interval as your paychecks—weekly forecasts if you are paid weekly, and monthly forecasts if you are paid monthly. Comparing income and spending forecasts allows you to judge whether your expected income will support all of the expenditures you expect to make. A forecast that indicates planned expenditures will exceed expected income alerts you to the need to reduce your planned expenditures while there is still time, otherwise you must either draw on your savings or bor-

Tip It is generally not wise to allow credit card balances to remain unpaid when you have ample savings available in the bank. Probably the rate you are paying on credit card balances is substantially higher than the rate you are earning on your savings. The difference is even greater when you consider that you must pay taxes on interest earned on savings, but you cannot deduct interest that is paid to a credit card company.

row to pay for the difference. You can decide which of these options is best suited to your particular circumstances. Starting a personal budget includes the tasks discussed below.

Estimating Your Income

Estimating your weekly or monthly income generally presents few problems, especially if you earn a salary or receive a pension that remains the same from one pay period to the next. Income is more difficult to forecast when you are paid an hourly wage for a job that entails uncertain hours. A workweek that typically varies between 20 and 50 hours makes it difficult to forecast how much you will earn next month, let alone how much you will earn during the same period next year.

The income portion of your budget should include the earnings of your spouse and income from savings accounts and other investments you may own. Only savings and investment income outside of retirement plans should be included as part of your budget. If gross income (your total salary or wage) is used for the budgeted earnings, be certain that all payroll deductions (withholding for federal and state taxes, Social Security, health insurance, etc.) are included in the expenditures section of the budget. An alternative method is to use your net pay, or take-home pay (i.e., the net amount of your paycheck after payroll deductions) for your earnings figure. This allows you to avoid always having to expense your payroll deductions.

Estimating Your Expenses

Personal expenses tend to be difficult to forecast, especially if you haven't been paying much attention to how your income is being spent. Expenses are difficult to estimate, partly because there are so many categories and subcategories of spending—groceries, medicines, restaurant meals, electricity, gasoline, newspapers, haircuts, lottery tickets, cable, and on and on. Do you spend money on 50 different items per week? A hundred? You probably don't have a clue. The great variety of expenditures makes it difficult to keep track of your current spending and to estimate your future spending.

The considerable monthly variation in many categories of spending is another reason expenses are difficult to forecast. Think how much your electric bill varies from month to month, and from the corresponding month last year. How about spending on clothing? Automobile repair? Prices of many food items are very volatile and especially difficult to forecast.

The first step in estimating what your monthly expenditures will be over the next year or two (or more) is to compile a fairly detailed record of your past spending patterns. Even though you haven't saved the receipts for all the goods and services you have purchased during the past several years, you probably have credit card statements and check registers that will provide much of the data required to reconstruct your spending. The total amount of your weekly or monthly spending can be estimated by subtracting the amount you have saved each period from the income you earned in the period. Keep in mind that some bills are paid after the date of purchase, so this method provides only an estimate, not an exact amount of spending.

Major expenditures are often fairly easy to estimate. The rent or mortgage payment, the automobile loan payment, insurance premiums, and several utility bills remain relatively constant from one period to the next. It is more difficult to develop a spending forecast for groceries, restaurant meals, clothing, and other types of spending that fluctuate from period to period. Still, an examination of your past spending patterns is a great help for estimating how you are likely to be spending your future income.

Making a Summary of Income and Spending Estimates

Each period's forecast for total income and total spending provides an advance look at whether you are likely to experience a surplus or a shortage of money during a particular budgeting interval. You can expect to be able to add to your savings, prepay some debt, or increase spending above planned levels dur-

Figure 21 ■ **Outline of a Personal Budget**

	January	February	March
Income Projections			
Salary	_____	_____	_____
Spouse salary	_____	_____	_____
Part-time work	_____	_____	_____
Interest from savings	_____	_____	_____
Dividends from stocks	_____	_____	_____
Total income	_____	_____	_____
Spending projections			
Rent	_____	_____	_____
Groceries	_____	_____	_____
Clothing	_____	_____	_____
Utilities	_____	_____	_____
Life insurance premium	_____	_____	_____
Auto insurance premium	_____	_____	_____
Home insurance premium	_____	_____	_____
Entertainment	_____	_____	_____
Miscellaneous	_____	_____	_____
Total spending	_____	_____	_____
Loan payments	_____	_____	_____
Surplus or Deficit (Total income less Total spending and Loan payments)	_____	_____	_____

> **Tip**
>
> Contact your creditors in the event you are having difficulty making your payments in a timely fashion. Many reputable lenders are willing to restructure your payments in order to allow you to fully repay your loan. It is not in a lender's interest to force you into bankruptcy.

ing periods when the forecast indicates that income will exceed spending. If the excess proves to be unusually large, you may be able to accomplish all three goals. On the other hand, you are likely to have to draw on your savings, borrow, or reduce spending below planned levels during periods when your expenditures are forecast to exceed your income.

Large, occasional expenses such as tax payments and insurance premiums might cause you to project deficits during several months each year. Occasional deficits are not particularly worrisome if they are offset by expected surpluses during other months. Ideally, your spending plans could be revised to reduce or postpone certain expenditures during the months when deficits are anticipated. Another, less desirable option is to plan to take out a short-term loan during the deficit months.

A forecast showing that planned spending will regularly exceed expected income is cause for genuine concern. Forecasts of continuing deficits call for major reductions in your spending plans (or a quick change of employment), unless you have accumulated a substantial stash of money that can be used to offset the planned deficits. If you are unable or unwilling to plan now for the changes that will bring your budget into balance (i.e., make your spending and income approximately equal), unwelcome changes will eventually be forced upon you when little maneuvering room is available. An outline for a personal budget is illustrated in Figure 21.

How a Personal Budget Improves Credit Management

A budget accounts for both cash and credit purchases, but in very different ways. Forecasts for cash transactions are entered in the budgeting period in which the respective purchases are expected to occur. If you anticipate spending $200 per month on groceries, enter $200 on the appropriate spending line for each of the months your budget covers. If you expect that grocery prices will increase by 10 percent during the coming year, add an additional $20 per month to next year's monthly budgeting periods.

How to Account for Credit Purchases in a Personal Budget

Credit purchases should not be entered in the expenditures section of your personal budget. Rather, you should enter only the payment or payments that you expect to be making to the lenders that financed the credit purchases. If you purchase a new car with the proceeds from a loan, your budget should show the monthly payments required by the loan agreement, not the purchase price of the car. The purchase price of the car does not represent a cash expenditure unless you pay in cash at the time of the purchase. Any down payment required by a lender will be included in your budget during the month the down payment is to be made. A personal budget utilizes cash income and cash expenses, and the only cash expenses relevant to a credit purchase are the down payment (if applicable) and the required payments on the loan that financed the purchase.

Suppose that 18 months ago you used the proceeds of a four-year loan to purchase a new car. The loan was scheduled for repayment with 48 monthly payments of $280, and 30 payments remain before the loan is fully repaid. The loan obligation resulting from the credit purchase should be included in your budget by listing the $280 expenditure for each of the next 30 months (see Figure 21). This assumes, of course, that you expect to keep the car until the loan is completely repaid. If you intend to continue driving the current car beyond the last scheduled loan payment, entries for the loan will fall to zero beyond 30 months, when loan payments cease. Continuing to drive a car beyond the date of the last loan payment does wonders for your personal budget by freeing up money for other uses. If you anticipate trading cars before the current loan is repaid, replace the $280 entry with a new, higher payment (you will need to estimate a payment amount based on the cost of the car you intend to purchase) beginning in the month you expect to trade.

Accounting for Multiple Loans

Individuals and families frequently find themselves having to make payments on several loans at a time. It is not unusual for a family to have a mortgage on their home, one or two car loans, a home-equity loan, and outstanding balances on one or more credit cards. New loans are periodically taken out at the same time that balances on existing loans are being reduced. With several outstanding loans, you end up managing a "loan portfolio" that is continuously being reduced and increased as existing loans are paid off and new loans are added. The ability to take on the responsibility of new debt payments is partly determined by success at repaying existing loans. You can feel comfortable purchasing a new automobile with borrowed money only when you have completely repaid the loan you made several years ago to pay for remodeling a bathroom.

If you have several outstanding loans and expect to undertake additional borrowing during the time covered by your budgeting system, payments associated with each loan should be entered on a separate line of your budget, as shown in Figure

Figure 22 ▪ Multiple Loan Entries in a Personal Budget

Loan Payments	January	February	March
Mortgage	$ 950	$ 950	$ 950
Auto loan (Chevy)	420	420	
Auto loan (Jeep)			380
Credit union (personal loan)	120	120	
Total loan payments	$1,490	$1,490	$1,330

This example assumes that the loan on the Chevy is fully paid by February, at which time money is borrowed to purchase the Jeep. The credit union loan is fully paid in February, so no payment is required in March.

22. The payments required by your home mortgage are listed on one line, payments for your auto loan are listed on a separate line, and so forth. Using separate lines for each set of loan payments makes it easier to identify the budgeting impact of each outstanding loan. While lumping all your loan payments together into a single monthly entry does permit you to determine if your total debt obligations, combined with other projected expenses, will exceed your projected income, it does not allow you to identify which particular loan(s) may be the primary cause of any potential problems.

Interpreting Budget Information Concerning Your Debts

A personal budget assists you in managing your credit by identifying the total amount of debt payment you can handle during any particular period. Knowing the upper limit of the loan payments you will be able to make may help you control your borrowing. Being forced to come to grips with the spending you will have to forgo in order to meet the payments on a loan is another factor that is likely to dampen your demand for credit. A personal budget forces you to consider this tradeoff, which economists call *opportunity cost*. Calculating the opportunity cost of taking out a loan weighs the required payments on the loan against the purchases the loan payments would restrict you from making.

Suppose you are debating whether to trade cars in several months. The car you want to purchase is relatively expensive, and the payments on a new four-year loan will run $520 per month, a substantial increase over the $280 you are paying on your current loan. To determine whether you can afford to trade cars and incur additional debt, rework your budget expenditure projections by substituting a $520 loan payment for the current $280 payment, beginning three months from the current month. The auto loan payments section of your personal budget will now include three monthly entries of $280 and subsequent monthly entries of $520.

The higher loan payment resulting from trading automobiles will cause no great financial strain if your budget has been projecting substantial monthly surpluses. Incorporating the higher loan payments into your revised budget projections should indicate a continuation of a surplus, although at a reduced level. This indicates that you should be able to handle the additional debt that results from trading vehicles. On the other hand, if you are currently forecasting several years of balanced budgets, an increased loan payment may cause a shift from a series of

---

Tip Using your home as collateral for a succession of loans is generally a bad idea, because you may end up at your planned retirement with so much debt that you cannot quit work. Make plans to have your home loan paid off several years before your planned retirement.

small monthly surpluses and deficits to a series of substantial monthly deficits.

What options are available when budget projections indicate you will be facing chronic monthly deficits? Failing to take action now will cause you to draw down your savings or, if sufficient savings aren't available, borrow additional money in order to be able to remain current on your car payments. The borrowing option means you will be taking out a new loan for the purpose of helping to pay an existing loan. This is a poor choice, because it means you are putting off a needed restructuring of your spending plans. It is also a sign that you are in serious financial trouble.

One obvious solution to an expected budget deficit is to forgo the new car and continue to drive your current vehicle. You might also consider purchasing a smaller car or a less costly used car that will require you to borrow less money. You can also investigate the possibility of financing the new vehicle for five years rather than four years. Extending the period of the loan for an additional year will reduce the amount of your monthly payments. Unfortunately, a loan with a longer maturity also prolongs the agony of making payments and restricts your

Figure 23 ■ Possible Courses of Action When Forecast Expenditures Exceed Forecast Income

- Increase your income by working more hours, adding a second job, or finding a better-paying job.
- Reduce planned spending in one or more budget categories.
- Refinance one or more loans to lengthen maturities and reduce monthly payments.
- Draw down savings.
- Borrow.
- Sell assets you own.

other spending for a longer period. An extended maturity also causes you to incur greater interest expenses over the life of the loan. Another course of action is to plunge ahead with the trade and plan to reduce other spending, something that is often easier said than done. It is one thing to rationalize that you will cut back on spending for utilities and groceries in future months, but it is something else again to actually do the cutting. Figure 23 includes some possible courses of action when your personal budget forecasts that expenditures will exceed income.

Personal Bankruptcy: The Last Resort

Attempting to solve financial difficulties with personal bankruptcy is a last-ditch solution that erects a legal barrier between you and your creditors while you attempt to sort out the dreary state of your finances. Bankruptcy isn't a no-cost solution, because you are likely to be forced to part with some of your assets before the process is complete. On the other hand, a bankruptcy filing won't require you to surrender everything you own. Your home, a vehicle that provides transportation to work, clothing, and certain other assets can often be retained in a personal bankruptcy proceeding. The particular assets you are legally able to keep depend in large part on the law of the state in which you reside.

Another important consideration is that bankruptcy will leave a blot on your financial record that is likely to cause reputable creditors to give you a wide berth for quite some time. Financial institutions often view a personal bankruptcy as proof that you are a poor money manager who chose to renege on your promises to creditors. Why should they expect something different in the future? Creditors will be aware of a bankruptcy filing through your credit file, where the information will remain for up to ten years. Two types of personal bankruptcy, summarized in Figure 24, are available to individuals.

The bankruptcy route to financial rescue was once reserved for individuals in desperate financial condition who were willing to endure the scorn of friends, relatives, associates, creditors, and nearly anyone else who learned of the bankruptcy filing. How times have changed. Today, bankruptcy is considered by many to be an acceptable step for persons who are unable or unwilling to live up to their financial commitments, even though individuals often abuse this escape hatch when they borrow large amounts of money with no intention of honoring their financial commitment. Although your friends and neighbors may not harbor ill will because of your bankruptcy (at least, not outwardly), you are likely to find that creditors who are willing to lend money at a reasonable rate of interest have a long memory.

Although personal bankruptcy should be a last resort when you are facing financial problems, there may come a point when you become so mired in debt that there is no possibility for escape, because creditors are clamoring for virtually all of your income. Perhaps this situation comes about because you or a family member has experienced a serious illness accompanied by overwhelming medical bills. The doctor and hospital bills may be so large that there is no possibility you can ever fully repay your creditors. Or, a major legal judgment resulting from an accident in which you are found at fault may force you to consider personal bankruptcy.

A bankruptcy filing keeps most creditors at bay until you are able to arrange some type of repayment plan that is acceptable to all the parties. The repayment plan can include an extension of your debts (i.e., smaller payments over a longer period of time), a reduction in the interest charges you must pay, or a

Figure 24 ■ Two Kinds of Personal Bankruptcy

Individuals or families typically file for bankruptcy because of large medical expenses, job loss, divorce, or credit abuse. In the event you become mired in debt and your creditors are uncooperative in agreeing to restructure your loans, bankruptcy may prove to be the only feasible alternative. Two types of personal bankruptcy are available, Chapter 7 and Chapter 11.

Chapter 7 Bankruptcy

- You must file a petition with the bankruptcy court with a list of all your assets and debts.
- State laws generally permit you to retain a home, clothing, tools of your trade, and a means of transportation. There is a limit on the value of each of these.
- Your creditors are likely to have to accept less than full repayment of their loans.
- Following the bankruptcy, you have no additional obligations to your creditors.
- Certain debts, such as tax obligations, alimony, child support, and student loans, cannot be settled in bankruptcy court.
- This type of bankruptcy can be used only one time every six years.

Chapter 11 Bankruptcy

- A court-appointed trustee uses your future earnings to repay your creditors.
- The repayment can occur over a three- to five-year period.
- Your creditors are likely to have to settle for only partial repayment of your debts.
- You are required to have legal representation to file.
- You are permitted to retain your assets.

Tip Debt collectors are not legally permitted to harass, oppress, or abuse you. You are permitted to sue debt collectors who violate this law.

Tip

To file a credit complaint or obtain information about credit issues, visit the Federal Trade Commission website at www.ftc.gov, or call toll-free 1-877-382-4357.

reduction in the amount of the debt you must repay. A bankruptcy filing does not affect your responsibility for child support, alimony, and certain types of taxes. Most experts strongly suggest that you seek help from an attorney (who is likely to require a cash down payment or, perhaps, payment in full) before filing your bankruptcy petition. You may find that you can negotiate a debt restructuring with your creditors without actually filing for bankruptcy. Many creditors find mention of

Figure 25 ■ Annual Consumer Bankruptcy Filings

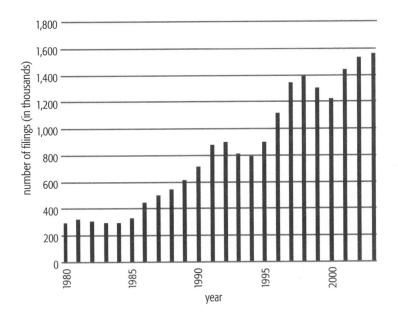

bankruptcy to be sufficiently threatening (they often have a lot of money to lose) that they will renegotiate the terms of a loan rather than face the uncertain outcome of a bankruptcy.

In truth, creditors often play an important role in creating personal credit difficulties. Overly aggressive merchants convince people to buy things they can't afford (merchants often don't know or care what their customers can afford, especially if the customers are paying with a credit card), and aggressive creditors allow people to borrow more money than they can reasonably be expected to repay. Overspending and excess borrowing eventually return to haunt creditors, who then may receive only partial repayment on their outstanding loans. Personal bankruptcies are more numerous during difficult economic times when unemployment is high. Figure 25 illustrates the upward trend in personal bankruptcies since 1980.

6 Credit Cards

Credit cards and their plastic cousins—automated teller machine (ATM) cards, debit cards, travel and entertainment (T&E) cards, and charge cards—are fast becoming the preferred method of payment for many types of transactions. For years people have used these cards to pay for travel-related purchases such as gasoline, lodging, airplane and rail tickets, and restaurant meals. More recently credit cards have gained popularity for buying personal items that in years past were typically purchased with cash or by check. Who imagined 20 years ago that virtually all grocery stores would accept credit cards? Credit cards have become virtually a necessity when ordering merchandise via telephone or on the Internet. Increasingly, credit, debit, and ATM cards are used to obtain cash from ATMs that remain open around the clock, rain or shine, 365 days per year. They never take a holiday and even remember to remain open an additional day on leap year. What a great idea—converting plastic into folding money.

The new uses and wider acceptance of plastic money have caused most people to consider it a necessity to carrying one or more credit cards. Some individuals have dozens of cards, many of which they seldom use. Have you attempted to rent a vehicle recently without being able to produce a credit card? How

Figure 26 ■ Revolving Credit Outstanding

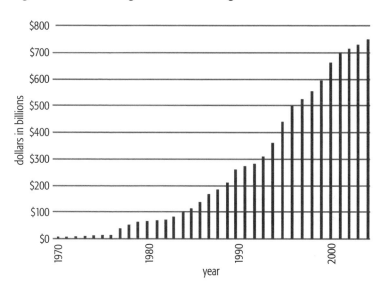

about checking into a hotel for a stay of several days? Plastic is power, at least until the monthly statements arrive. Figure 26 provides a look at the soaring use of consumer credit.

How the Cards Work

Credit cards, charge cards, debit cards, and T&E cards can be used to purchase goods and services at business establishments that accept the particular type of card you have. The cards are used as replacements for payment by cash or check. The merchant who accepts your card for payment remits the charge electronically to the card company, which then reimburses the merchant for 95 to 98 percent of the dollar amount that is submitted. The issuer of the card retains the remaining 2 to 5 percent as a service fee. The size of the fee charged by the card issuer depends on the merchant's type of business and the dollar amount of charged purchases the merchant submits for reimbursement. Small merchants have the least negotiating power and generally pay the highest fees. This is a reason small businesses may not be particularly pleased when you want to pay by credit card. Some economists contend that merchants cover credit card service fees by raising the prices of the goods and services they sell. If this theory is correct, even consumers who choose to pay with cash end up paying higher prices when they buy goods and services from merchants who accept payment by credit card.

Some businesses accept several different cards for payment, while other businesses are more selective and accept only one or two cards. For example, most merchants accept both Visa and MasterCard. Some also accept other cards, including Discover and American Express. Some retailers, although not many, accept only their own card. If you want to make a purchase from a business that accepts Visa or its own card and you have only a MasterCard, too bad. You better have cash or a spare check. This is unusual, but it does occasionally happen. A significant number of businesses do not accept any form of payment other than cash (including, in most cases, by check), primarily because they do not want to pay the service fees charged by the card companies. At present few fast-food restaurants or movie theaters accept payment by credit card, although this is changing. Many small businesses accept only cash or checks. You cannot use cards to pay your insurance premium or most taxes. Credit cards can be used to pay federal income taxes, but only by paying an additional fee so that the government doesn't get shortchanged on the amount of its tax receipts. A business with no competitors has less incentive to accept cards for payment.

> **Tip** Streamline the inventory of credit cards that you hold. Holding multiple credit cards makes it more likely that you will charge more and suffer the accompanying credit difficulties. In addition, using multiple credit cards makes it more difficult to keep track of what you owe and when it is due. Having more cards also makes it easier to misplace or lose a card, possibly without even missing it.

Types of Cards

While the term *credit card* is often used in a generic sense to identify any card that can be used for making purchases, the term more properly identifies a card that possesses certain characteristics. Actually, some cards frequently referred to as credit cards don't provide access to credit at all. It is important to understand the differences among different types of cards so that you will be able to make an informed choice regarding the type of card that is best for you.

The chances are that you will be able to enjoy all the benefits provided by credit cards by holding a single national credit card. Having only one card facilitates maintenance of records by keeping monthly statements and bills to a minimum. The fewer bills you receive, the less likely you are to forget to pay one of them. In addition, more charges on a single card will identify you as an important customer of the issuer. Being an important customer means your complaint, plea that a fee be removed, or request for a lower interest rate is likely to receive a more sympathetic hearing.

Credit Cards

Credit cards such as MasterCard, Visa, Optima, and Discover allow users to charge purchases at merchants or draw cash advances from financial institutions and ATMs. The dollar amount of each purchase accumulates in a balance that is scheduled for full or partial payment once a month. Finance charges are levied on accounts that have not been paid in full by each statement's due date. Finance charges for cash advances generally begin accumulating from the date of the cash advance. A credit card can be used as often as you like so long as the outstanding balance on your account does not exceed a predetermined maximum (your credit line) established by the card's issuer. You may want to request an increase in your credit line if you tend to make substantial credit purchases that regularly bump against the maximum. A credit limit increase shouldn't be a problem if you have a record of paying your bills in a timely manner and enjoy an income level that can support a higher level of debt. Most credit cards have separate credit line restrictions for purchases and cash advances. For example, an account with a $5,000 credit limit on purchases may specify a $1,000 limit on cash advances.

Some financial institutions issue *secured credit cards*—cards that carry a credit line equal to the amount of money you have on deposit at the institution. Funds in your account secure your obligation to the issuer and can be used to cover any bills you fail to pay. Secured cards are generally of interest only to individuals who have a poor credit history (or no credit history) and are unable to qualify for a regular credit card. An expanded discussion of credit cards follows this section.

Debit Cards

Debit cards, issued by many of the same financial institutions that issue credit cards, can be used to pay for purchases or to obtain cash advances, but the amount of a purchase is immediately deducted from your checking account at the financial

> **Tip**
>
> A cash advance on a credit card is a convenient way to obtain money, but it can be quite expensive. Be certain you understand any fees that may apply to a cash advance on your credit card. Try to save this option for emergencies when no other sources of cash are available.

institution that issued the card. Debit cards offer convenience (you don't have to carry cash or bother to write a check) but no credit, thus the different name. Although generally offered without a fee, debit cards initially failed to gain popularity with consumers because of the need to have funds available in order to use the cards. These cards have received increasing acceptance in recent years following heavy promotion by issuers who collect fees from merchants but don't have to give credit to users. Using a debit card is essentially the same as writing a check, only more convenient. Merchants will often ask if you wish to use your card for a credit card purchase or a debit card transaction, because it is less expensive for the merchant to process debit card transactions.

Travel and Entertainment (T&E) Cards

T&E cards such as those issued by American Express (American Express also issues credit cards) can be used to pay for purchases from merchants that accept them, although these cards are accepted at fewer establishments than are credit cards. Unlike credit cards that allow you to carry unpaid balances into subsequent months, T&E accounts must be paid in full each month. Thus, T&E cards give you an extra 30 to 50 days before you are required to come up with the money to pay in full for the purchases you charged, but they don't allow you to extend payment further, even at the cost of paying an interest charge.

Charge Cards

A charge card can be used to purchase goods and services at the business that issued the card. Petroleum companies (Shell, BP, ExxonMobil) and many retail chains (Sears, Target, and JCPenney) issue charge cards, in part to build customer loyalty. Charge cards do not involve an annual fee and are generally easier for an individual to obtain than are national credit cards. Other than the severe restriction on where these cards can be used, charge cards function much like credit cards. Cardholders who pay their monthly bill in full avoid finance charges. Partial payments result in unpaid balances that cause finance charges to be added. Finance charges on charge cards are often substantially higher than on many credit cards. Charge cards have lost popularity as issuers of these cards increasingly accept national credit cards.

ATM Cards

Like debit cards, ATM cards do not provide a user with access to credit. Rather, these cards allow you to make cash withdrawals from your checking account at thousands of ATMs around the world. ATM cards offer the convenience of allowing one to obtain cash at any time and at many locations, but they have nothing to do with credit. Withdrawals from an ATM owned by someone other than the card issuer often entail a fee, which may be substantial when calculated as a percentage of the amount withdrawn.

Characteristics of Credit Cards

Credit cards all provide the same basic function of allowing you to purchase goods and services and to obtain cash, but they have varying benefits and costs. Credit card companies sometimes offer a variety of benefits—such as free travel insurance, travel discounts, frequent-flier miles, cash rebates, free hotel rooms, free merchandise, and collision insurance for car rentals—in order to convince consumers to apply for and use their cards. All the issuers are searching for an edge to attract and retain customers in what has become a very competitive market. Differences among issuers can be significant, so you need to watch out for your own interests in selecting a credit card. Figure 27 presents an overview of what credit card companies must disclose to applicants for their cards.

Cardholder Liability

In the event your credit card is lost, stolen, or used by someone else without proper authorization, you are normally responsible for charges to a maximum of $50 per card. Any liability on your part assumes that have been previously informed of this liability (read the fine print). You will generally not be held responsible for any unauthorized use of your credit card if you immediately report a lost or stolen card by phoning a number listed on your

Figure 27 ▩ Information a Credit Card Company Must Disclose

When you apply for a credit card, the card issuer must either disclose directly, in the form of a table with headings, or tell you how to obtain the following information:

- The annual percentage rate (APR) for purchases made on credit.
- How the annual percentage rate is determined if it is a variable rate.
- The method used to compute the balance for purchases against which the finance charge is imposed.
- The amount of any minimum finance charge.
- Any transaction fee for purchases, whether a specific dollar amount or percentage fee.
- Transaction fees for cash advances and fees for paying late or exceeding the credit limit.
- The amount of any type of annual fee you will be charged.

> **Tip**
>
> Hotels and rental car companies often contact your credit card company to request a "hold" or "block" equal to their estimated charge. The block will be released a day or two after checkout, but only if you pay with the same card used to guarantee the payment—pay with a different card, and the block on the card used to guarantee payment may be in effect for up to two weeks. If you pay with a different card, request that the block be removed from the card that was used for the guarantee.

statement. Your liability for unauthorized use of a debit card (if you have one) can be substantially larger than the liability for a credit card. The $50 liability limit applies to a debit card only if you report the loss of the card to the credit card company within 2 business days of discovering the loss. In the event the 2-day limit is missed, you can be held responsible for up to $500 in unauthorized charges. You can be held liable for unlimited unauthorized use if you fail to notify the card company within 60 days of unauthorized charges appearing on your statement. Issuers of cards may offer reduced cardholder liability as a benefit. For example, an issuer may offer zero liability on unauthorized purchases to holders of a particular type of card.

Charges to Cardholders

Credit cards are made available because the cards are intended to produce a profit for the financial institutions that issue them. In fact, these cards have become so profitable for many financial institutions that an increasing number of associated companies have been recruited to assist in the battle for customers. Holiday Inn, AT&T, General Motors, and Ford Motor Company have all associated their brand name and their customers with issuers of credit cards. Intense competition among card companies has produced some good deals for consumers, but you need to understand your own credit needs and know what features to look for in order to make a wise choice among the hundreds of cards that are available.

Annual fees   Some card companies charge cardholders an annual fee that typically ranges between $25 and $100. Issuers sometimes offer two or more classes of cards, including a regular card, a premium card, and a super-premium card, each with different annual fees. An annual fee is generally charged to a cardholder's account on the initial statement and on each subsequent renewal date. Credit card issuers that charge an annual fee will sometimes forgive or reduce this fee, but only if you ask. The better a customer you are, the more likely the fee will be forgiven. The annual fee can be avoided if, within 30 days of receiving the statement that includes the fee, you notify the card company that you wish to cancel your card.

Competition has forced many credit card companies to eliminate or reduce the annual fees they charge cardholders. The financial institutions that offer these cards haven't reduced their fees to be good guys, but rather to attract new applicants and increase renewals among current cardholders, who regularly receive solicitations from competing financial institutions. A list of credit card companies that do not charge an annual fee regu-

Tip   Don't pay extra for a gold card, a platinum card, a titanium card, or even a plutonium card if you are unlikely to use its touted advantages. These premium cards are often designed to appeal to your ego rather than provide real benefits.

larly appears in several publications, including each weekly issue of *Barron's* and each monthly issue of *Money.* You are likely to find several advertisements from card issuers in Sunday newspaper supplements. Credit card companies earn income from charges to merchants who accept the cards (i.e., discounts on reimbursements) as well as interest income received from cardholders who do not pay their balances in full each month. In other words, issuers do not need to charge an annual fee in order to make a profit on your account.

Other fees Credit card companies levy several miscellaneous fees that should be investigated when you are choosing a card. With competition forcing reductions in interest rates and annual fees, card issuers are increasingly looking to other types of fees as a profit center. As a result, these other fees have increased in both size and number. It is very important that you understand the fees an issuer can charge.

- Card companies sometimes charge a fee for issuing more than one card per account. This charge is fairly unusual and isn't important if you need only a single card, but it should become a consideration if you require additional cards for your spouse and college-age children.

- A penalty is likely to be assessed if the outstanding balance on your account exceeds the credit limit that has been granted by the issuer. Requesting a credit limit increase may help avoid this fee, but making use of a higher credit limit is more likely to leave you overextended.

- Card companies typically levy a fee for cash advances. The fee may involve a flat charge of from $1 to $10 per transaction, or a percentage fee of from 1 to 5 percent of the money you obtain. Fees are sometimes different for cash advances obtained from inside a bank compared to advances obtained from an ATM (you figure out why).

- You may be assessed a fee for a balance transfer. The fee may be either a fixed amount or a percentage of the balance transferred. The fee may vary depending on whether you choose to transfer a balance over the telephone, on the Internet, or by a check supplied by the issuer. One major issuer charges 3 percent of the cash advance, with a $5 minimum and a $50 maximum fee.

- You will generally be assessed a fee if you pay less than the required minimum payment or if you pay later than the due date indicated on your statement. The late fee is in addition to interest that is computed on your unpaid balance. These fees are particularly important if you are a poor organizer or forget to make payments in a timely manner. Figure 28 offers some suggestions for avoiding credit card late fees.

Finance Charges on Credit Card Accounts

Both interest rates and the method by which interest charges are calculated vary among credit card companies. Fortunately, card companies must disclose the interest rate they charge, along with the method they use to calculate the finance charges that are

> **Tip** Credit card issuers often levy an additional charge of 1 to 2 percent on foreign transactions. Before traveling overseas, check with your credit card issuer to determine if any additional fees are imposed on foreign transactions. If so, search for another issuer that does not charge extra for foreign transactions.

Figure 28 ■ Avoiding Credit Card Late Fees

Late fees have experienced substantial increases, to the point that a late fee may exceed the monthly interest charged on your account balance. Thus, it is important, at least, to pay the minimum required payment each month and to get your payment to the credit card company by the specified date. Here are some steps you can take to make certain you don't get hit with late fees:

• Carefully read the payment rules. Different issuers have different rules regarding payment.

• Use the return envelope and billing statement provided by your credit card company.

• Send payment at least one week prior to the date the payment is due. This should be sufficient allowance for any postal delays.

• Pay bills online. Some issuers allow you to schedule payments for up to a year in advance. Online payment is especially valuable if you are nearing a due date, although most firms recommend you pay two or three business days prior to the due date. Paying online saves you a stamp.

• Pay by phone if you must make a last-minute payment. The credit card company will need your checking account number and bank routing number, both of which are printed on the bottom of your checks. Some credit card companies charge for this service.

• Consider wiring your payment or using an overnight delivery service. The fee charged by these services is likely to be less than the charge for a late payment—plus, paying late may result in an increase in the interest rate charged on your account.

• Call the credit card company if it is the first late charge and you have a good credit record. This is especially effective if your payment is late by only a day or two. The credit card company is likely to waive the late fee, but not on a regular basis. Be persistent when you talk with a representative.

---

added to your account. Unfortunately, the method of calculation is nearly impossible for most cardholders to understand.

Credit card companies typically allow a grace period of 20 or 25 days beyond the billing date, during which time you can

> **Tip**
> Several methods can be used for calculating interest charges on credit card balances. If you tend to carry balances on your account, it is important to choose a card from an issuer that uses a method favorable to you. The method of calculating interest is unimportant if you regularly pay your entire balance by the payment date.

avoid interest charges by paying the full balance of your account. If a credit card company with a 25-day grace period bills you on January 5, you have until January 30 to pay the full amount of the bill without incurring an interest charge. As long as you continue to pay each new monthly balance in full by the due date, you will not be required to pay any interest. A long grace period is to your advantage because it provides you with a longer time to pay your bill without having interest charges posted to your account. Unfortunately, grace periods have been getting shorter among most card issuers. A few card companies offer no grace period, which means these companies begin charging interest as soon as credit purchases are posted to your account. You should make every effort to avoid using a credit card that provides no grace period for payments.

The High Cost of Credit Card Interest

With the exception of temporary promotional rates, credit card companies tend to charge relatively high rates of interest on unpaid balances. This isn't always true, but it is generally the case. There is some justification for the relatively high interest charges, as it is expensive to operate a credit card business. Consider the simplicity of making home loans in which a single loan for $100,000 or more will often remain in effect for 15 or 20 years. The lender either sells the loan or sits back and lets the

Tip Try not to make major credit card purchases just before the closing date on your account. Making purchases just after rather than just before the closing date will give you an additional four weeks before you have to make payment. The closing date will be printed on your statement and will remain approximately the same from month to month. Call the credit card company if you are unable to locate the closing date on your statement.

checks roll in (unless, of course, the borrower quits paying). Compare this with a credit card operation in which huge numbers of charges and reimbursements—often for relatively small amounts of money—are made every day. Resolving the many cardholder complaints concerning improper charges, shoddy merchandise, late payments, lost cards, late receipt of statements, and so forth is a labor-intensive and expensive proposition. And what about all of the money lost by card companies because of fraud and nonpayment by cardholders? Overextended cardholders flee to bankruptcy court or simply quit making payments. Thieves steal credit cards and credit card numbers to make charges that are never paid.

The majority of credit card companies calculate interest charges using a fixed rate of interest that changes only infrequently. Even though short-term market rates of interest are constantly on the move, interest rates charged on most credit cards change by only small amounts, if at all. Interest rates charged on credit card balances are usually quite high during weak economic periods, when market rates are relatively low. During a period of very high market rates of interest, interest rates charged by credit card companies may actually seem reasonable.

Some financial institutions charge variable interest rates on credit card balances. The interest rate charged on the unpaid balances of these cards is generally equal to the prime rate (the interest rate that commercial banks charge their most credit-worthy borrowers) plus 2 to 7 percent, depending on the policy of the particular card company. The spread between the prime rate and the rate charged is often dependent on the cardholder's credit history. Cards with variable rates offer relatively low finance charges (compared with cards with fixed rates) during periods when market rates of interest are low, and relatively high finance charges during periods when market rates of interest are high. The risk in having a card with a variable interest rate is that short-term interest rates may experience a major increase during the period your account is running a big balance. Pay your balance in full each month and it won't matter whether the interest rate is fixed or variable, because you won't be paying any interest.

How Finance Charges Are Calculated

Credit card companies calculate the finance charges added to monthly statements by applying a periodic interest rate to the outstanding balance in a cardholder's account. As we shall see, several methods are used for determining the balance in an account that is subject to interest charges. The periodic interest rate is calculated by dividing the annual percentage rate by the

Tip If you are unable to pay off large credit card balances, pay as much as possible and switch to a card with a low annual percentage rate. Lists of low-interest-rate credit cards are available in several personal finance magazines and on the Internet at www.cardlocator.com and www.bankrate.com.

number of billing periods in a year, generally 12. Thus, an annual percentage rate of 15 percent converts to a periodic rate of 15 percent divided by 12, or 1.25 percent per period when finance charges are calculated monthly. The dollar amount of the monthly finance charge is calculated by multiplying the periodic interest rate by the appropriate balance.

The method used to calculate the balance in an account that is subject to interest charges is very important in determining the finance charges that will be added to the account. If you consistently pay your balance in full and on time, you will not normally incur any finance charges, unless the financial institution that issues your card does not permit a grace period. On the other hand, if you regularly carry outstanding balances on your card (i.e., you always owe money to the card company) and, as a result, incur finance charges every month, the method for computing your balance is crucial, because it can make a big difference in how much you will have to pay for credit.

Adjusted balance The balance at the beginning of each billing cycle is adjusted downward for payments you made during the same cycle, but the balance is not adjusted for purchases you made during the cycle. The date the financial institution receives your payment does not affect the balance that is used for calculating finance charges as long as the payment is posted during the billing cycle. The adjusted balance method of calculating your outstanding balance is most favorable from your standpoint, because it results in the smallest balance, and therefore the smallest finance charge.

Average daily balance In this method of calculating finance charges, the balances in your account during each day of the billing cycle are added together, and the result is divided by the

Figure 29 ■ Calculating the Average Daily Balance and Finance Charge

Credit card issuers typically use the average daily balance, including new purchases, when calculating a monthly finance charge. The following is a typical account with several purchases and one payment during the month in which the finance charge is calculated. The account carries a balance of $3,500 during each of the first three days, at which time a new purchase of $500 brings the total balance to $4,000. The balance remains at this level for the next ten days, when another purchase of $400 raises the balance to $4,400. A single payment of $1,400 is made seven days later, causing the balance to drop from $4,400 to $3,000. Five days later an additional $1,500 is borrowed, resulting in an outstanding balance of $4,500 that remains to the end of the month. The average daily balance during the month is calculated by dividing the sum of the balances in the right column by the number of days in the month. The finance charge is calculated by multiplying the average daily balance by the monthly interest rate (one-twelfth of the 12% annual rate, or 1%).

Number of Days	Account Balance	Number of Days × Account Balance
3	$3,500	$ 10,500
10	4,000	40,000
7	4,400	30,800
5	3,000	15,000
5	4,500	22,500
30		$118,800

Average daily balance = $118,800 ÷ 30 days = $3,960
Finance charge = 0.01 × $3,960 = $39.60

number of days in the cycle. In calculating the average daily balance, payments you make during the cycle are subtracted from the amount you owe. New credit purchases that are posted to your account during the cycle may be included in the calculation. Most, but not all, credit card companies include new credit purchases when calculating the finance charge for your account. It is to your advantage if the credit card company does not include new purchases in calculating the balance subject to the periodic interest rate, because the resulting balance will be lower than if new purchases were included. The method used to calculate the average daily balance is described in Figure 29.

Two-cycle average daily balance   The balances in your account during each day of the last two billing cycles are added together, and the sum is divided by the number of days in the two billing cycles. The average daily balance is then multiplied by the periodic interest rate to determine the finance charge for the month. Payments you make during the two billing cycles are subtracted in calculating the average, but new purchases may or may not be added to the balance, depending on the credit card company's method of calculation.

Previous balance   The periodic interest rate is applied against the beginning balance of your account to determine the month's finance charge. No payments or credit purchases made during the month are included in the calculation.

Ending balance   The monthly finance charge is calculated by multiplying the periodic interest rate times the balance at the end of the billing period. The timing of payments and purchases is unimportant, since only the final balance is used to calculate the finance charge.

Cardholder Freebies

Many card companies offer a variety of benefits at no charge in order to attract and retain cardholders. The benefits vary from one card company to the next and often among different cards issued by the same financial institution. Issuers sometimes require that you qualify for a premium card (sometimes at a higher annual fee) to receive the extra benefits. Whether the benefits offered by a card company hold much value for you depends on your own particular needs. You may find that a few of the added benefits offered by a card company are actually quite useful while other benefits have little value. If you are unlikely to use any of the extra services, you should be able to locate cards that have fewer bells and whistles but offer lower interest rates and/or annual fees.

Extended warranties Extended warranties typically double the manufacturer's warranty for up to one additional year. Thus, if the manufacturer provides a 90-day warranty, the credit card company will provide an extra 90 days of warranty protection when the issuer's credit card is used to purchase the item. The warranty extension is normally limited to one extra year, so if the regular warranty is for two years, the credit card company's extension will provide warranty protection for a total of three years. An extended warranty for no additional cost is a valuable benefit.

Collision and comprehensive vehicle insurance damage waiver protection Some credit card companies provide rental car collision and comprehensive insurance so that you can decline the costly insurance coverage offered by the rental car company. Of course, you must pay for the rental with the card that offers the insurance in order to benefit from the coverage. Insurance provided by credit card companies is secondary to the coverage of your own automobile insurance policy. Insurance coverage provided by a credit card issuer is a valuable benefit if you occasionally rent vehicles, especially when your regular insurance doesn't cover damage to a rental vehicle.

Emergency assistance Credit card companies sometimes provide cardholders with emergency medical and legal assistance and emergency cash. Emergency assistance mainly benefits individuals who do a lot of traveling and are likely to end up in places where they don't know anyone and can't speak the local language.

Affiliation benefits Some financial institutions have an arrangement whereby a particular organization is rewarded for your use of a special credit card. For example, a credit card issuer might agree to donate a few cents to your college alma mater each time you use the card to pay for a purchase. Likewise, you might choose a card that is affiliated with an environmental organization of which you are a member. Affiliation cards generally have a relatively high annual fee, a high interest rate, or both. You may notice that advertisements for affiliation cards seldom mention the meager amount that affiliated organizations receive from the use of these cards. Don't ask why.

Merchandise, frequent-flier miles, and cash rebates Airlines were among the first organizations to affiliate with credit card companies that offered frequent-flier points to their cardholders. These cards nearly always entail an annual fee and award one frequent-flier point per dollar charged. Credit card companies also offer free hotel nights, merchandise, and cash rebates to cardholders who achieve prescribed levels of charges. These cards can be a great deal for individuals who tend to charge a lot of purchases and pay their monthly account balance in full. Beware of high rates of interest if you tend to carry balances from month to month.

7 Automobile Loans

Vehicle loans are a major source of revenues and profits for many lenders. Banks, savings and loans, credit unions, finance companies, and vehicle dealers and manufacturers have all been attracted to the business of offering credit to vehicle purchasers. Automobiles, trucks, and sport utility vehicles (SUVs) serve as desirable collateral for loans even though they are mobile and occasionally disappear. An active secondary market in used vehicles allows lenders to repossess and easily dispose of automobiles and trucks in the event a borrower fails to make required loan payments. Lending experience and regularly published data from an active used car market permit lenders to accurately estimate the fair market value of the vehicles both when they are first purchased and during their useful lives. Being able to accurately value collateral allows a lender to determine how much money can safely be loaned and how long the loan should last.

The short maturities of most vehicle loans are an attraction for many lenders who want the money they have loaned to be returned relatively quickly. Short- and intermediate-term loans help protect a lender from the numerous things that can go wrong over long periods, and the relatively short time involved allows lenders to more accurately forecast factors that affect a loan's profitability and risk. Market rates of interest (which affect the lender's cost of funds), inflation (which affects the purchasing power of loan payments received by the lender), and the market value of collateral are all important considerations for lenders.

Short- and intermediate-term loans are also desirable because of a reduced likelihood of deterioration in a borrower's ability to service his or her debts. The longer the time until a loan is to be repaid, the greater the chance there will be a decline in a borrower's financial strength and cash flow (e.g., the borrower divorces, contracts a serious illness, or becomes unemployed). Changes in a borrower's financial status can occur over the short term, of course, but major changes are less likely than for periods of many years.

Characteristics of Automobile Loans

Automobile loans generally stipulate monthly payments for a period of three, four, five, or six years, depending on the term that is offered by the lender and chosen by the borrower. Vehicle loans can range up to eight years, but this length is unusual, and is generally restricted to the purchase of luxury vehicles. Required payments on an automobile loan may be fixed or adjustable, depending on whether the loan is made at a fixed or variable interest rate. The lender retains the title to the vehicle during the term of the loan to make certain that the borrower cannot sell the vehicle being used as collateral before the loan is fully repaid. The vehicle title is eventually turned over to the borrower at the time of the final loan payment.

A borrower who falls behind in making the required loan payments runs the risk that the lender will assume possession and sell the vehicle. It is not unknown for lenders to dispatch employees (recovery specialists) in the dark of night to recover vehicles from delinquent borrowers—who are not likely to be happy. This is dangerous work! The recovered cars are then offered for sale to individual buyers or through wholesale auctions. Most lenders are not interested in operating a car lot and prefer not to repossess a vehicle on which they may well lose money in a quick sale. Thus, if there is a reasonable chance a loan can be salvaged, lenders will often go out of their way to work with a borrower who has fallen behind on a loan obligation. On the other hand, lenders don't want to be placed in a position of having their collateral decline in value at the same time that interest is accumulating on an overdue loan. A borrower remains responsible for any part of the outstanding loan balance that remains after a repossessed vehicle is sold. The lender is obligated to return to the borrower any proceeds from the disposal that exceed the balance remaining on the loan.

The Amount That Can Be Borrowed

Lenders prefer to structure a loan (i.e., establish the down payment, loan length, and payment size) so as to ensure that the market value of the collateral is greater than the outstanding balance on the loan. Because automobiles normally experience a steep decline in value during the first several years of owner-

> **Tip**
> If default on a car loan is looming, you may be better off selling the car yourself and paying off the debt. A creditor is allowed to repossess your vehicle without notice any time you are in default. If the car is repossessed, you may have to pay the full balance due, plus towing and storage costs, to get it back. If you can't pay, the creditor may sell the car.

ship, most lenders are reluctant to lend the entire purchase price to a buyer. It is not unusual for a lender to allow someone to borrow a maximum of 80 to 90 percent of an automobile's purchase price, although the percentage can go higher. The larger the proportion of the purchase price a lender is willing to finance, the more interest the lender expects to earn, but the more money the lender stands to lose in the event it becomes necessary to repossess and sell the vehicle. Lenders that have low down payment requirements tend to attract the borrowers that are most likely to default on a loan. Hence, a smaller down payment is likely to be accompanied by a higher interest rate.

The larger the proportion of a vehicle's purchase price you borrow, the more finance charges you will be required to pay over the life of the loan. The higher finance charges stem both from a larger amount of money borrowed and the likelihood that a loan with a smaller down payment will probably carry a higher interest rate. An $18,000 loan requires 50 percent more in finance charges than a $12,000 loan that has the same interest rate and term. Choosing to borrow a smaller proportion of an automobile's purchase price may allow you to negotiate for a lower interest rate because of the improved position of the lender, who is less likely to suffer a loss on the loan in the event the vehicle must be repossessed. An added advantage of making a large down payment is that you will be unable to fritter away

Tip Consider making a large down payment or paying cash for a vehicle if you have significant savings available. Using savings rather than taking out a loan could save several thousand dollars in interest charges.

your savings on something else, since the money will be tied up in the automobile.

Length of a Loan

Most automobile loans are for terms of three, four, or five years, but some lenders now go as long as eight years, while other lenders forgo even five-year loans. The length of automobile loans has crept upward as vehicle prices have increased and lenders have sought to keep monthly payments within the reach of more families. It is not necessarily in a lender's interest to make five- and six-year loans, because the longer term increases the likelihood that the outstanding balance on a loan will exceed the market value of the vehicle being used as collateral. Collateral valued at less than the balance on the loan places the lender in an unfavorable position if it becomes necessary to repossess and sell a vehicle being used as collateral.

Unfortunately, relentless price increases for new and used automobiles have resulted in fewer vehicle buyers being able to afford the payments required on three-year loans. Figure 30 illustrates the relatively steady increase in the maturity length of new car loans. In the early 1970s, new car loans averaged approximately three years, while the same loans in more recent years are slightly over five years. Paying $222 per month for three years to borrow $7,000 to buy a $9,000 car is one thing; paying $668 per month to borrow $22,000 to buy a $26,000 SUV is another story, especially considering that the payments must come from your after-tax income. Remember, interest paid on automobile loans is not a deductible expense in calculating federal income taxes. Rather than reduce the size of the payments by lowering the interest rates they charge (not likely!), most lenders choose to achieve the same result by lengthening the term of the loans, which, in turn, increases the number of

> **Tip** Interest rates on loans to purchase used cars are generally higher than interest rates on loans to buy new cars. The lower cost of credit to buy a new vehicle is not as important as the higher annual depreciation you are likely to suffer from buying and owning a new vehicle.

payments required of borrowers. Lengthening the $22,000 loan from three years to five years decreases the monthly payment from $668.28 to $425.32. Choosing to add yet another year and taking out a six-year loan will reduce the payment to $364.60.

Choosing a loan with a longer payback will indeed reduce the required monthly payment, but a longer term also increases the

Figure 30 ■ Maturity Length of New Car Loans

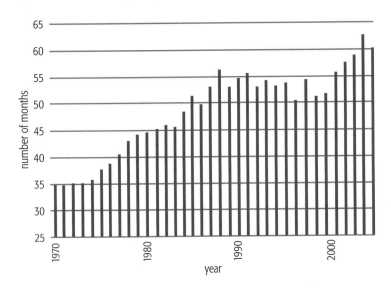

Figure 31 ■ Finance Charges for Automobile Loans of Different Lengths

	Loan Length			
	3 Years	**4 Years**	**5 Years**	**6 Years**
Amount borrowed	$22,000	$22,000	$22,000	$22,000
Interest rate	6%	6%	6%	6%
Monthly payment	$668.28	$516.67	$425.32	$364.60
Total payments	$24,058	$24,800	$25,519	$26,251
Total interest paid	$2,058	$2,800	$3,519	$4,251

dollar amount of interest that will be paid. Figure 31 illustrates differences in interest charges for loans with different maturity lengths. The $22,000 loan used in the example results in total interest charges of $3,519 when a five-year loan is chosen. Interest charges fall by nearly $1,500 to $2,058 if a three-year payoff is selected. As long as you are confident you can handle the payments, you should choose a loan with a short maturity to save on interest charges. Consider also that a lender may bump up the annual interest rate for loans with a longer maturity. In other words, a five-year loan is likely to carry a slightly higher interest rate compared to a three-year loan.

Tip If the purchase of a new vehicle requires that you take out a six- or seven-year loan in order to be able to afford the payments, you probably should consider purchasing a less costly vehicle that will allow you to choose a three- or four-year loan.

Interest Rates on Automobile Loans

Although interest rates charged on new automobile loans fluctuate in sympathy with changes in market rates of interest on other types of credit instruments, they change relatively slowly. Interest rates on Treasury securities and corporate bonds, the prime rate charged for short-term loans to creditworthy customers, and rates on mortgage loans all have an impact on the interest rates that financial institutions charge on automobile loans. If expectations for increased inflation or tightened credit availability cause an increase in market interest rates, the interest rates lenders charge on automobile loans will also increase.

The interest rate charged on automobile loans is affected by market interest rates because market rates affect both how much a lender must pay to attract money from savers and the income that can be earned by making other types of loans. The higher the rate a financial institution must pay to savers, the higher the rate the institution will attempt to charge on the loans that it makes. Falling interest rates cause a decline in a financial institution's cost of money that is likely to result in a reduction in the rate the institution charges on vehicle loans. A decision to change the interest rates charged on these loans will also depend on the actions of competing lenders.

How the Interest Rate Affects Your Payment

A higher interest rate charged on any type of loan of a given size and length results in larger periodic payments. Suppose you decide to purchase a $26,000 SUV with a $4,000 down payment, thus requiring a loan of $22,000. Figure 32 illustrates the monthly payments, total payments, and total interest cost for several interest rates on three-year and five-year loans. If you choose a five-year loan at an annual rate of 5 percent, the monthly payment will be $415.17. The same loan made at a 6.5

Figure 32 ■ Finance Charges on Loans with Different Interest Rates

	Interest Rate				
	4.5%	**5.0%**	**5.5%**	**6.0%**	**6.5%**
Three-year loan					
Amount borrowed	$22,000	$22,000	$22,000	$22,000	$22,000
Monthly payment	654.43	659.36	664.31	669.28	674.28
Total payments	23,559	23,737	23,915	24,094	24,274
Total interest paid	1,559	1,737	1,915	2,094	2,274
Five-year loan					
Amount borrowed	$22,000	$22,000	$22,000	$22,000	$22,000
Monthly payment	410.15	415.17	420.23	425.32	430.46
Total payments	24,609	24,910	25,214	25,519	25,828
Total interest paid	2,609	2,910	3,214	3,519	3,828

percent interest rate will require monthly payments of $430.46, an increase of approximately $15 each month for five years. The small increase in monthly payments caused by a relatively large increase in interest rates results from the short-term nature of the loan. Payments on a short-term loan go mostly to reducing the outstanding loan balance rather than to paying interest charges. On the 5 percent loan, the initial $415.17 monthly payment has $91.67 allocated to paying interest and $323.50 to reducing the principal. Subsequent payments will have increasing amounts allocated to reducing the principal. By comparison, the initial $430.46 payment on the 6.5 percent loan will have $119.17 going to interest and $311.29 to principal reduction.

The nominal change in payment size that results from a relatively large change in the interest rate is one reason that consumer borrowing for automobile purchases is not greatly affected by interest rate changes. Consumers considering an automobile loan tend to be influenced more by the size of the payments they will be required to make than by the interest rate they are charged. As an informed borrower, however, you should be aware that even a relatively small payment increase is likely to amount to a substantial amount of money over time. For example, the 6.5 percent loan noted above will result in nearly $1,219 in extra interest charges over the five-year life of the loan as compared with the same loan at 4.5 percent interest. The additional cumulative finance charges caused by a higher interest rate are even greater for a six- or seven-year loan.

Fixed versus Variable Interest Rates

Some, but not all, lenders offer automobile loans at both fixed and variable interest rates. A loan with a fixed interest rate locks you into a constant monthly payment for the life of the loan, while a loan with a variable interest rate involves adjustments in both the interest rate and the payments at scheduled intervals, usually annually or semiannually. Constant payments have the advantage of being easier to budget, because you know exactly how much money must be paid each month. An adjustable-rate loan is more difficult to budget (although this type of loan typically includes limits on the amounts by which interest rates and payments can be increased), but it may have the advantage of smaller overall finance charges. Choosing between fixed-rate and variable-rate loans depends on the initial interest rate difference and your expectations regarding interest rates over the next several years. An expectation of rising interest rates should

Figure 33 ■ The Real Deal: Zero Percent Financing

Zero percent financing became the rage in the early 2000s as automobile manufacturers aggressively competed for business. The bargain in financing was made possible by historically low short-term interest rates—meaning that the money being given away by the auto companies wasn't costing them very much. The zero percent deal was indeed a deal for those who were fortunate enough to qualify. The problem was that zero percent loans were sometimes limited to two- or three-year loans that, even with zero interest, resulted in monthly payments too high for many potential buyers to afford. In addition, the zero percent loans often required a spotless credit record. Potential buyers who had a spotty credit record or required a five- or six-year loan were out of luck.

cause you to favor a fixed-rate loan. In fact, choosing a fixed rate is the less risky choice, because you pin down both the payment size and loan length.

Refinancing Automobile Loans

A significant decline in market interest rates after you have made a commitment on a fixed-rate loan may make looking into refinancing your loan worthwhile. Refinancing means that you use the proceeds of a new loan to pay off the balance on an existing loan. Refinancing provides an opportunity to reduce the interest cost of financing your car when interest rates have fallen enough that interest savings will more than offset the trouble and fees of making a new loan. Refinancing mortgages has long been a popular activity of homeowners, who stand to save substantial interest charges on large loans with long repayment periods. Refinancing a vehicle loan offers more modest savings and is most feasible in the early stages of a loan. Potential savings are greater the longer the time to the payoff. Still, if interest rates fall several percentage points within the first or second year of your loan, you may discover that you can refinance and lower your monthly payments by $20 or so. If you are thinking about refinancing, make certain that interest savings will not be more than offset by substantial fees paid to the lender. Also make sure that reduced payments on the new loan will not ensue primarily from a loan extension (i.e., you are required to make more payments) rather than a lower interest rate. You may be able to save on fees by informing your current lender that you are thinking about refinancing at a lower rate offered by another lender. Your current lender may offer the same deal with lower fees.

Leasing as an Alternative to Borrowing and Buying

A growing proportion of new auto sales are being financed with leases rather than loans. Automobile dealers increasingly choose to advertise lease payments rather than loan payments and/or vehicle prices, and no wonder! Dealers have found that customers who lease a vehicle have greater dealer loyalty than customers who purchase a vehicle. Even more important, a lease appears to be a less expensive method of obtaining the use of a vehicle compared with the loan payments that would be required to finance the purchase of the vehicle. The payment difference between leasing and borrowing is especially noticeable for luxury vehicles that cost $30,000 and more. Are the advertised lease payments too good to be true? Perhaps.

Who Owns the Vehicle When the Payments End?

Lease payments are indeed lower than the corresponding loan payments that would be required to purchase the same vehicle. Most current leases, however, leave ownership of the leased vehicle with the lessor (the financial institution that owns the vehicle and collects the lease payments), rather than the lessee

Figure 34 ■ Open- versus Closed-End Leases

Financial institutions write two types of vehicle leases. The two types of leases differ with regard to who owns the vehicle at the termination of the lease and who bears responsibility for more rapid than expected depreciation in the market value of the leased vehicle during the term of the lease.

Open-end lease. An open-end lease holds you, the lessee, responsible for any difference between the projected residual value of the vehicle and its actual market value at the end of the lease period. The projected value of the leased vehicle will be included in the lease agreement you sign. If a leased vehicle depreciates faster than anticipated, you will be required to pay the difference between the expected value and the actual market value at the termination of the lease. Suppose a monthly lease payment is based on the assumption that a vehicle will have a $6,000 resale value at the end of the lease. If the market value turns out to be only $4,000, you will be required to come up with the $2,000 difference if you have entered into an open-end lease. Abuses and consumer misunderstandings and complaints caused Congress to pass legislation in the late 1970s limiting the maximum amount a lessee must pay on an open-end lease. Open-end leases continue to be offered, although they have mostly been replaced by closed-end leases.

Closed-end lease. A closed-end lease (sometimes called a *walkaway lease*) specifies the price at which a lessee may purchase a vehicle at the termination of the lease. No purchase is required of a lessee, who can walk away from the vehicle and enter into a lease for a new vehicle. A closed-end lease shifts the risk of overestimating the residual value of a leased vehicle to the lessor, who agrees to absorb losses that stem from rapid depreciation. A closed-end lease frees you from worry about being required to come up with additional funds at the termination of the lease to pay for unanticipated depreciation in the leased vehicle. A closed-end lease does hold you responsible for above-normal wear or mileage.

(the party that uses the vehicle and makes the lease payments), at the termination of the lease. This type of lease usually requires two to four years of monthly payments (the number depends on the terms of the lease), and it generally permits, but does not require, you to purchase the car from the lessor at the end of the lease at a price stipulated in the lease agreement. Although the payments on a loan used to finance a vehicle purchase are typically higher than comparable lease payments, a loan allows you to remain the owner of the vehicle following your last payment.

The distinction of who owns the vehicle at the end of the required payments is the major reason for the differences between loan payments and lease payments. A lease payment is largely a function of the expected decline in the market value of the vehicle (i.e., the depreciation) during the term of the lease. A vehicle that is expected to retain an unusually large portion of its original purchase price should have a relatively low lease payment relative to the retail price because the lessor will retain possession of a car that can be sold at a favorable price at the termination of the lease. By contrast, a vehicle that typically loses a large portion of its market value in the first few years of ownership is likely to have relatively large lease payments to compensate the lessor for this expected loss in value.

Who Should Lease?

Most leases are convenient, ongoing financial arrangements whereby you sign a two-, three-, four-, or five-year lease, drive the vehicle for the allotted time, return the vehicle to the lessor at the termination of the lease, and repeat the process with a new vehicle and a new lease. Leasing doesn't allow you to build any equity (ownership value) in a vehicle; at the same time, it does free you from worry about both depreciation and trading

> **Tip**
>
> Don't make the mistake of choosing a lease only because the monthly payment is less than for a loan to purchase the vehicle. Remember, you will not have a vehicle at the end of a lease, but repaying a loan will result in your owning the vehicle. Monthly lease payments are less than loan payments because the lessor will regain possession of the vehicle when the lease payments are complete.

vehicles. Depreciation, the major expense of owning a newer model car, is the concern of the lessor, not the lessee, although lease payments are established by the lessor at a level that is expected to recover any loss in the market value of the vehicle being leased. A lessor who overestimates the future value of a vehicle is likely to establish a lease payment that is too low. This is to your benefit as a lessee.

A lease is most appropriate if you regularly trade for a new vehicle every two or three years. Leasing allows you to move from one vehicle to another without being required to negotiate a trade or come up with a large down payment. On the other hand, if you ordinarily keep a car for six or seven years or even longer, your best bet is probably to finance the purchase with a loan (or with savings). Financing a car with a three-year loan will allow you to drive the vehicle an additional three or four years free of loan payments. The reprieve from $400 or $500 in monthly car or lease payments provides breathing room to take care of other financial matters, such as adding savings to a retirement fund or paying off other loans. Owning is likely to be especially advantageous if you take very good care of your car and you don't drive a lot of miles. Your car should last longer and have above-average value when you decide to trade.

Some Important Things You Should Know about Leasing

Leasing is an alternative method of acquiring the use of a vehicle. Don't make the mistake of moving up to a more expensive automobile just because the lower lease payment (as compared to a loan payment) fits into your budget. Remember that the entire process must be repeated from scratch at the termination of a lease. In this respect, leasing an automobile is like renting a home: Both involve lower payments than ownership, and neither leaves you with anything when the lease terminates.

The lessor's profit Lease payments are established at a level to provide a return on the lessor's capital that is tied up in the leased vehicle. In other words, the lessor purchases the vehicle and expects a reasonable return on the investment. The lower the return a lessor will accept, the more you should benefit.

Qualifying Normally you must have a good credit record to qualify for a lease. A lease with a low down payment places the lessor at greater risk of suffering a substantial loss in the event you default on a lease obligation.

Getting the best deal You should shop aggressively for a lease, just as you would shop among dealers for the best price on a car and among financial institutions for the lowest rate on a loan. Both financial institutions and automobile manufacturers will sometimes offer special leasing deals.

Breaking a lease Terminating a lease early will negate all of the calculations regarding residual value and the lessor's expected return. Lessors normally charge a substantial penalty in the event you decide to terminate a lease prior to the scheduled termination date. Sign a lease agreement only if you are prepared to fulfill the terms of the lease.

Mileage Leases typically specify a maximum number of miles you can drive a vehicle without getting hit with an excess-mileage charge. A lease typically allows 15,000 miles annually before an extra charge is imposed. You should attempt to negotiate for a higher allowance when you expect to exceed the mileage stipulated.

Taxes Sales taxes, if applicable, are ordinarily added to each lease payment. You are also responsible for paying certain other taxes and fees, such as title, license, and registration.

Down payment Most vehicle leases require a nonrefundable down payment, usually $1,000 or so, depending on the value of the vehicle being leased. The down payment may be substantially higher, in which case the lease payment will be reduced. You may also be required to put up a security deposit (generally refundable). Substantial down payments and security deposits make the leasing option more expensive and less desirable.

The Best Choice: Paying with Your Savings

Your best bet from a financial standpoint is to purchase a vehicle for cash. Being able to implement this alternative isn't easy, but it certainly isn't impossible. Paying cash allows you to avoid the interest charges, fees, and monthly payments of a loan or a lease. It also saves you from the effort it takes to shop for a loan or lease with the most advantageous terms. On the negative side, purchasing a vehicle for cash depletes your savings and commits your funds to an asset (the vehicle) that will almost certainly decline in value.

The choice of whether to use your savings or choose a loan or lease should depend, in large part, on the rate of return you expect to earn on your savings compared with the rate of interest you will be required to pay a lender. As a general rule, you should choose the borrowing route if you can earn a higher after-tax return on your savings than the bank will charge on a loan. If you are unlikely to earn a return that is comparable to the interest rate you will be charged on a loan (or the interest rate in the lease), you should use your savings to buy a vehicle.

Suppose your savings are currently earning an annual return of 4 percent and you expect to continue earning approximately the same rate for the next several years. After paying taxes at a rate of 25 percent on income from the savings, you earn an after-tax return of 3 percent (the remaining 75 percent of the 4 percent annual return after taxes have been paid). If lenders are currently charging from 6 to 7 percent annual interest on four-year automobile loans, you are better off financing a car purchase by drawing on your savings rather than by taking out a loan. This assumes, of course, that you have accumulated sufficient savings to pay for the car. It also assumes that paying cash for a vehicle will not deplete your savings to a dangerous level. Figure 35 illustrates the monthly savings required to accumulate $20,000 at various rates of return and over the three most common maturities for vehicle loans. For example, accumulating $20,000 in four years would require monthly savings of $384.85 if you are able to earn an after-tax return of 4 percent. Delaying the goal by one year to five years would allow you to reduce the monthly savings requirement to $301.60.

One effective method for accumulating adequate savings is to regularly set aside a predetermined amount of money into a fund specifically designated for the purchase of a vehicle. The required contributions into the fund depend on three factors: the return you expect to earn on your savings, the length of time before you intend to purchase the vehicle, and the amount of money you wish to accumulate. The higher the price of the vehicle, the sooner you intend to purchase the vehicle, and the

Figure 35 ■ Monthly Savings Required to Accumulate $20,000

After-Tax Return on Savings	Savings Period		
	36 months	48 months	60 months
2%	$532.49	$400.55	$317.20
3%	531.57	392.65	309.34
4%	523.73	384.85	301.60
5%	515.97	377.16	294.00
6%	508.29	369.57	286.53

lower the return you expect to earn, the greater the monthly contribution you must make.

Setting aside adequate savings sounds great, but how can you go about saving money for your next car purchase when you are still paying for the vehicle you are currently driving? This amounts to making double payments—one each month on the current car loan and another each month for the car you are planning to purchase next. How about driving your present car an additional year or two after paying off the current loan? If you bought your current car two years ago with the proceeds of a three-year loan, bite the bullet and plan to drive the car three more years. During the two years following repayment of the current loan, continue to make the same payments into a savings fund for your next car purchase. Even though you may be unable to accumulate enough savings in two years to pay the entire cost of a new car, the pool of money will enable you to make a large down payment that substantially reduces the loan payments required for your next car purchase. In fact, one more cycle and you should be sufficiently ahead of the game to pay cash for your next car purchase.

Home Loans

Buying a home is synonymous with borrowing money—big time! A house (or, for many families, a series of houses) is the single most expensive thing you are likely to purchase during your lifetime (although you may cumulatively spend more on automobiles, SUVs, and pickup trucks), and the loan to finance the purchase will consume a major portion of your income for 15 to 20 years, or longer. This is serious borrowing! A home loan involves such a large amount of money for such a long period that you need to understand all of your options so that you will know what you are doing when you get ready to borrow.

Why Buy a Home?

Most homebuyers have several motives that lead them to shell out tens of thousands of dollars for a down payment; pay additional thousands of dollars in fees to attorneys, an appraiser, and a lender; and sign a commitment to make substantial monthly payments for the next 200 to 300 months. Mostly, homebuyers are searching for a place to hang their hat, store their valuables, and raise their families. After all, you have to eat and sleep somewhere, and it may as well be a place where you are comfortable. Homebuyers generally view a home as an investment that will appreciate in value and provide tax benefits. Although this is often a secondary motive for buying a home, for most people, the investment aspect plays an important role in determining the style, size, and location of the home they purchase. For example, you are likely to choose a home that you expect will be easy to resell, especially if you are likely to relocate in several years. Perhaps you desire a home that lets others know how financially successful you have become. After all, big wheels generally live in big houses.

A Home as an Investment

Economists who measure and interpret economic data for the federal government classify home construction as investment spending rather than as consumption. Individuals and families have much the same view of home ownership—a home is not just a place to live, but also an investment that can be expected to increase in value. The market value of a home is affected by a number of factors, including local economic activity, population shifts, land availability, and general inflationary pressures.

From an investment standpoint, a home should be considered one component of a portfolio that includes savings accounts, stocks, certificates of deposit, a pension, mutual fund shares, and other investments you may own. A home is a tangi-

---

Tip It is worthwhile to spend substantial time and effort shopping for a home loan. The large dollar amount being borrowed, in conjunction with the 15- to 25-year length of a home loan, means that huge savings can result from a relatively small reduction in the interest rate. Locating a lender that charges fewer points can also result in substantial savings.

ble asset with investment characteristics that provide a balance to the financial assets that comprise a substantial part of most individual investment portfolios. During inflationary times, for example, home values generally increase, whereas some financial assets often tend to perform poorly. Bond values increase during deflationary periods when home prices are likely to stagnate or decline. Common stocks are best suited to an economic environment with stable prices.

The Tax Advantages of Home Ownership

A major financial advantage of home ownership is the opportunity for a considerable reduction in federal and state income taxes. Having a mortgage loan to finance a home purchase can save you thousands of dollars in taxes annually because of tax laws that favor home ownership. Mortgage interest and property tax payments can be entered as itemized deductions when you calculate your taxable income. Deductions for mortgage interest and property taxes reduce taxable income if, when combined with other allowed deductions (e.g., charitable contributions, state and local income taxes, and certain medical and employment expenses), they cause your total itemized deductions to exceed the standard deduction. The amount of tax savings you gain from owning a home also depends on the tax rate applicable to your income: the higher the rate at which your income is taxed, the greater the tax savings you reap from mortgage-interest and other deductions.

How Much Home Can You Afford?

Although newspaper and magazine articles about home buying often include rules of thumb for determining the maximum amount you should allocate to housing, there are no hard-and-fast rules that apply to everyone. The size of your income is

Figure 36 ■ **How Interest Rates Affect the Size of Mortgage Payments**

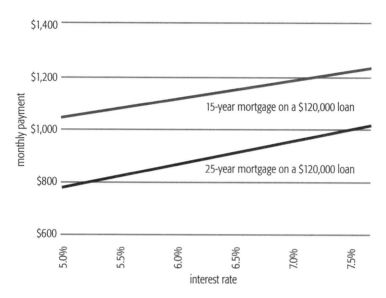

obviously important; as is the amount of funds you have available for a down payment. The stability and certainty of your income is another consideration—committing yourself to an extended series of costly expenditures is a risky proposition if your current employment and income are uncertain. Determining how much of your income to devote to home ownership requires that you consider other priorities and obligations: funds for an emergency, health insurance, adequate life insurance, and so forth. The size of your family will play a central part in determining how much of your income is consumed by expenditures on food, transportation, and so forth, and how much will be available for housing.

The interest rate you must pay on a mortgage loan is an important determinant of how expensive a home you will be able to purchase. A high interest rate results in large monthly payments that make it more difficult to service a given amount of debt. Borrowing $140,000 at a 5 percent interest rate is one thing; borrowing the same amount at 7 or 8 percent is something else. The interest rate is of less importance if you have saved enough money to make a substantial down payment. Figure 36 illustrates how the size of the monthly payments on a loan is influenced by the interest rate that is charged. Payments for both a 15-year loan and a 25-year loan are shown.

The amount of home you can afford is partly a function of the importance you attach to home ownership. Some families consider owning a nice home to be so important that they are willing to forgo vacations, new cars, eating meals out, and many of the things that other families consider necessities. Two similar families with identical incomes and financial assets but different spending priorities can spend significantly different amounts on housing.

Owning a home, especially an older home, is likely to require substantial cash outlays in addition to the monthly loan payments. Home ownership carries with it annual property taxes that are likely to amount to thousands of dollars and insurance coverage that is becoming increasingly expensive, especially in areas subject to natural disasters. Ask Florida homeowners near the Gulf or Atlantic coasts about how their insurance premiums have changed over the last several years.

Maintenance can be another major expense, especially as a home grows older. Appliances break, roofs leak, wood needs painting, yards need mowing, carpets need replacing, driveways crack, and the beat goes on. If you currently own a home, you are probably already coping with these headaches. Maintaining a home in top-notch shape requires physical effort and substantial monetary expenditures.

Importance of the Down Payment

The down payment you are able to make plays a major role in determining the amount of home you are able to buy and the size of the loan payment you will have to make. If you are interested in purchasing as expensive a home as possible (perhaps you wish to impress your mother-in-law, who said you would never amount to much), a large down payment will allow you to borrow a greater amount of money. Of course, you must be able to service the monthly loan payment that is required by a large loan. On the other hand, if you have already picked out the home you wish to purchase, a large down payment will allow you to borrow less money and will let you choose a loan with either a shorter maturity or smaller monthly payments. You are also likely to benefit from a lower interest rate, because a large down payment means the lender's loan is more secure.

Assuming that you have the funds available to make a large down payment, is this an advisable course of action? If you decide to purchase a $160,000 home, should you make the $8,000 (5 percent) minimum down payment required by the lender, or should you plunk down $32,000 (20 percent) or even $40,000 (25 percent)? The answer, of course, depends on just how much money you have available to make a down payment. It also depends, in part, on the return you expect to be able to earn on your funds compared with the interest rate you will be paying on the loan. If you consistently earn an annual return of 8 to 10 percent on your investments at the same time that you can borrow money for a home purchase at 6 percent, you should put down as little as possible so that you can maximize the amount of money you have available for investments. On the other hand, if you are a conservative investor who keeps a large proportion of your wealth in a money market account, certificates of deposit, or Treasury bills, you are unlikely to earn a

Figure 37 ■ **Effect of Down Payment on Monthly Payment and Overall Interest Cost**

Down Payment	Monthly Payment	Total Payments	Total Interest
$ 8,000 (5%)	$960.74	$345,866	$193,866
16,000 (10%)	910.18	327,665	183,665
24,000 (15%)	859.61	309,460	173,460
32,000 (20%)	809.05	291,258	163,258
40,000 (25%)	758.48	273,053	153,053
48,000 (30%)	707.92	254,851	142,851

Note: Based on the purchase of a $160,000 home with a 6.5% loan for 30 years.

return on your investments that exceeds the interest rate you will be required to pay on a home loan. In this instance you should favor making a substantial down payment to reduce your interest expense. Figure 37 illustrates the degree to which the size of a down payment affects the interest cost over the life of a home loan. Notice that a down payment of 25 percent rather than 10 percent results in interest savings of approximately $30,000 over the 30 years of payments. Interest savings from a larger down payment depends on the life and interest rate of the loan. A higher interest rate and longer maturity results in greater savings from a large down payment.

It isn't a good idea to drain most of your financial resources in order to make a large down payment on a home, even if your savings is earning only a relatively modest return. Hold back a portion of your liquid assets to finance an emergency fund. You also want to have funds available to take advantage of particularly good buys that occasionally come your way. It doesn't make sense to take all your liquid financial resources to make a large down payment on a home and then run up balances on a credit card account with a high interest rate. Choose a down payment that doesn't leave you financially strapped.

Financing the Purchase of a Home

Available financing will play a major role in determining how expensive a home you can purchase. The more restrictive lenders become in granting loans and the higher the interest rate they charge, the less financing you will be able to obtain and afford. If you are actively seeking to purchase a home, it is worthwhile to contact many lenders regarding the types and costs of loans they are making. You can often gain a head start by searching the Internet (http://www.bankrate.com is a particularly good site) and examining the business section of a local newspaper. Many major newspapers publish a weekly summary of the rates being offered by local financial institutions on a variety of loans and savings instruments. Mortgage loans are frequently available from sources you may overlook. For example, securities brokerage firms and mortgage brokers are likely to be good sources of mortgage loans. Check the yellow pages of your local telephone directory if you are unsure as to whether any of

> **Tip** If your local newspaper does not publish mortgage rate surveys, call at least five or six lenders for information about their interest rates, points, and fees. Mortgage information, including mortgage rates available in your region, is also available on the Internet at www.bankrate.com.

these lenders are located in your community. In fact, you might want to call most or all of the mortgage lenders listed in the yellow pages. A slightly better deal can often result in substantial savings on a large sum of money over the course of 20 to 30 years.

Seller Financing

Sellers are sometimes willing to finance all or a portion of the price of a home, often at a very favorable interest rate. Seller financing is most common when interest rates are high, conventional financing is difficult to obtain, and potential buyers are scarce. Borrowing from the seller is likely to result in reduced fees and a lower interest rate compared to borrowing from a financial institution. Sellers are sometimes willing to provide supplementary financing for a buyer who is unable to come up with the difference between the selling price and the amount a financial institution is willing to lend. Perhaps you are interested in purchasing a home selling for $120,000, but you have only $10,000 available for a down payment. Several lenders have indicated they will lend a maximum of $95,000, meaning that you must somehow come up with $25,000 of your own funds. The seller may agree to accept $105,000 immediately ($95,000 from proceeds of the loan plus your $10,000) along with a note for $15,000 from the seller that you will repay in monthly or annual installments over ten years. Depending on how badly a seller wishes to dispose of a home, you may be able to negotiate several financing alternatives, including a favorable interest rate.

Conventional Financing

Most lenders offer several types of mortgage loans. The choice you make will affect the size of your payment, the fees you must pay, and the interest rate you are charged.

Conventional loan The most common type of mortgage loan specifies a fixed interest rate and a constant monthly payment, generally for 15, 20, 25, or 30 years. Financial institutions typically lend a maximum of 75 to 80 percent of a home's appraised value on a conventional loan, meaning that you must come up with a down payment for the remaining 20 to 25 percent. A smaller down payment requirement may be offered if you agree to purchase insurance that guarantees the lender against loss. The insurance will require that you pay monthly premiums that are added to your payments. As described in Figure 38, you will probably want to request that this insurance be dropped after several years of payments.

The down payment required when you take out a mortgage loan protects the lender from a loss in the event you are unable or unwilling to keep your end of the bargain and make the monthly mortgage payments in a timely manner. A substantial down payment would allow the lender to recover the outstanding balance on the loan even if the home had to be sold for less

Figure 38 ■ Saving on Mortgage Insurance

Individuals who put less than 20% down on a home purchase are frequently required by the lender to pay monthly premiums for private mortgage insurance (PMI). This insurance protects the lender in the event the borrower defaults on the loan. The PMI on home mortgages signed after July 28, 1999, must be automatically terminated when a homeowner's equity reaches 22% of the home's original property value, if the mortgage payments are current. The PMI also can be canceled, at the request of the borrower, when equity reaches 20% of the original property value. Terminating PMI can save a borrower many thousands of dollars over the life of a loan. Mortgages signed prior to July 29, 1999, are not subject to this rule, but it is still worthwhile to ask that PMI be canceled once equity in a home exceeds 20%. Some states have laws that apply to early termination or cancellation of PMI, even if loans were signed prior to July 29, 1999.

than the purchase price. What's important to the lender is that the home not be sold for less than the outstanding balance on the loan.

Fixed monthly payments on a conventional loan are comprised partly of interest and partly of principal. If you select a 25- or 30-year mortgage, payments made in the early years of the loan will go mostly to cover interest being charged on the loan. Suppose you borrow $90,000 for 30 years at an annual interest rate of 8 percent. The loan requires a $660 monthly payment in order to reduce the balance to zero at the end of 30 years. Of the first $660 payment, $600 goes to pay interest (one-twelfth of 8 percent times $90,000) charged by the lender, and the remaining $60 reduces the outstanding balance on the loan to $89,940. The next monthly payment covers the second month's interest of $599.59 (one-twelfth of 8 percent times the new balance of $89,940) and reduces the loan's principal by $60.41. By the end of the second month, you have made two payments totaling $1,320 and reduced the principal on the loan by only $120.41! Cheer up—at least the interest you are paying is generating a heck of a tax deduction.

FHA-insured loan Borrowers unable to make the required down payment for a conventional loan may choose to have a loan insured by the Federal Housing Administration (FHA). The FHA has established standards both for homes and for borrowers to qualify for the insurance. There is a limit on the amount you can borrow with an FHA-insured loan and also with a VA-insured loan (discussed in the next section). Borrowers who qualify must pay the FHA an insurance fee to guarantee that the lender will not suffer a loss in the event the borrower is unable to fulfill the terms of the mortgage loan. FHA-insured loans generally require relatively small down payments that range from 3 to 5 percent of the appraised value, the main selling feature for this type of financing.

VA-guaranteed loan The Veterans Administration (VA) guarantees home loans for veterans of the armed forces. A VA loan guarantees a lender against a loss in the event a home is repossessed and sold for less than the loan's outstanding balance. The guarantee allows lenders to require little or no down payments on these loans, because the VA, rather than the lenders, absorbs the loss in the event a home must be sold for less than the balance on the loan. Homes must meet certain construction standards to qualify for a VA loan, and limits are placed on the amount of money that can be borrowed.

Adjustable-rate mortgage An adjustable-rate mortgage, or ARM (also called a variable-rate mortgage), incorporates a changeable interest rate that is tied to some standard, such as the Treasury bill rate, or to some index of rates, such as the cost of funds index. The rate of interest charged on an ARM can change at predetermined intervals (generally, annually or semiannually, as specified in the loan contract) if a change occurs in the associated rate or index. Lenders often prefer to make ARMs because these loans transfer the risk of changing interest rates to borrowers. With a fixed-rate loan, you are charged the same interest rate and make the same payment over the life of the loan no matter how much market interest rates change after the loan is finalized. You know the exact monthly payment you will be making 15 years (or more) in the future. Lending money at a fixed rate of interest can place the creditor in a bind if interest rates subsequently rise, causing an increase in the lender's cost of funds. A variable-rate loan allows the lender to charge an interest rate that varies with the lender's cost of funds. This is a "no-lose" proposition for a lender, but it offers danger to a borrower, who may find that monthly payments are substantially increased over a period of years.

An ARM will generally offer a lower initial rate of interest than a fixed-rate mortgage, because short-term interest rates (the rates that establish the interest rate charged on an ARM) are generally lower than long-term interest rates. The risk to you is that interest rates will rise after you borrow the money, thus causing an increase in the rate you are charged on the loan, along with a corresponding increase in either the size or the number of payments you must make. ARM loans include specified limits, called caps, on how much interest rates can change over specified intervals and over the life of the loan. For example, a loan contract may specify that the interest rate cannot change by more than 2 percent in a given year and cannot change by more than 4 percent over the life of the loan. Some ARM loans are, for a fee, convertible into fixed-rate loans, although usually at slightly higher interest rates than available to other borrowers.

Graduated-payment mortgage A graduated-payment mortgage provides for relatively low mortgage payments in the early years of a loan, to be followed by gradually increasing payments in subsequent years, when it is anticipated that your income will be larger and you will be financially able to handle bigger expenses. Payments in the early years of this type of loan are often lower than the interest being charged, causing the outstanding balance of the loan to increase. The monthly payments on a graduated-payment mortgage may be scheduled to increase each year, or at predetermined intervals such as every three years or every five years.

Tip An adjustable-rate mortgage may offer a lower initial interest rate, but it can subject you to substantial risk because the interest rate can experience substantial change over the life of the mortgage. An increase of several percentage points can raise monthly payments by over a hundred dollars.

Growing-equity mortgage This type of mortgage is designed for homebuyers who desire to pay off their loan early. Payments are scheduled to increase by a specific amount each month, causing principal to decrease more rapidly than would occur with fixed payments. With a growing-equity mortgage, a 30-year loan may be repaid in 15 to 20 years, depending on how rapidly payments are scheduled to increase.

Reverse mortgage A reverse mortgage allows a homeowner who has no outstanding mortgage to enter into a borrowing agreement whereby the lender provides the homeowner with a series of payments (loans) over a period of years. A reverse mortgage is primarily designed to allow someone who experiences difficulty meeting living expenses (normally a retiree) to gradually withdraw the equity in a home. This type of loan is likely to experience increasing popularity in future years as the number of retirees surges. Reverse mortgages are discussed in more detail at the end of this chapter.

Home-equity loan Home-equity loans have greater similarity to credit card accounts and other types of revolving credit than to mortgage loans. These specialized loans are primarily used by homeowners who seek funds to pay for purchases unrelated to home ownership—a vehicle, a vacation, medical expenses. Why is this, you ask? Because the interest you pay on a home-equity loan can be deducted from taxable income when calculating federal and state income taxes, while interest paid on credit cards and personal loans cannot. Also, a home-equity loan is likely to offer a lower interest rate compared with the rate you would pay on personal loans, especially credit card accounts. The maximum amount you can borrow on a home-equity loan is generally 70 to 80 percent of the appraised value of the home less the outstanding balance on your first mortgage. Essentially, a home-equity loan allows you to borrow against the equity of your home. For example, suppose a number of years ago you borrowed $100,000 to purchase a $120,000 home. The loan has now been paid down to $85,000, and the home has appreciated in value to $135,000. Your equity in the home is now $50,000, the difference between the market value of the home and the balance owed on the loan. Thus, the line of credit on a home-equity loan is likely to be limited to $40,000, or 80 percent of your current equity.

The great danger of a home-equity loan is that you will be tempted to borrow against your home for all kinds of purchases you would not ordinarily make. A home-equity loan allows you to buy more expensive clothes, take longer vacations, purchase an additional vehicle, and eat out more frequently at nice restaurants. Writing checks that immediately add to your loan balance provides access to the line of credit created by the home-equity loan. If you have difficulty controlling your spend-

> **Tip** When evaluating a home-equity loan, compare the offerings of at least three or four reputable lenders. Consider both the quoted interest rate and the annual percentage rate (APR) that includes other costs such as origination fees, discount points, mortgage insurance, and other fees.

> **Tip**
>
> Interest often isn't the only cost associated with a home-equity loan. A lender may charge a one-time application fee plus an annual fee of $50 to $75 to maintain the line of credit. You may also be charged a nonusage fee if you do not draw on the line of credit.

ing, a home-equity loan can cause you to be up to your eyeballs in debt as you head into your retirement years.

Points

Lenders often charge a one-time fee based on a percentage of the amount of the loan. Stated as *points*, this fee has the effect of increasing the cost to you and increasing the return to the lender. One point is equal to 1 percent of the amount you borrow. If you borrow $85,000 from a lender that charges 6.5 percent plus 2 points, you will pay an up-front charge of $1,700 (2 percent of $85,000) in addition to interest and all other expenses. Points charged on a mortgage loan do not affect the loan's annual percentage rate, although they certainly affect the cost of credit to you. On the plus side, points can generally be utilized as a deduction in calculating your income taxes. The deduction is subject to restrictions if the loan is for the purpose of refinancing.

You are likely to find that a lender is willing to negotiate with respect to both the interest rate and the points that are charged on a loan. For example, a lender may offer you the option of choosing a 6.5 percent loan with no points, a 6.25 percent loan with 1 point, or a 6 percent loan with 2 points. Your choice between fewer points or a lower interest rate will largely be influenced by how long you expect to live in the house. If you intend

Tip Negotiate for the fewest points as well as the lowest interest rate when shopping for a mortgage. A reduction of one point on a $100,000 mortgage will save $1,000.

to stay for many years, you are likely to be better off choosing a lower interest rate and paying the points that are a one-time expense. If you plan to move soon, you should generally avoid paying points and accept a higher interest rate. You must consider how much an extra point can buy in interest savings.

Additional Fees

Home loans generally entail expenses in addition to interest charges. Fortunately, most are one-time expenses charged at the time the loan is finalized. On the other hand, if the initial expenses are rolled into the mortgage, you will be paying them over the life of the loan. Fees you are likely to be charged at the time you finalize a loan on a home (called the closing) include a loan application fee, a loan origination fee, a credit report, an appraisal fee, a real estate transfer tax, a notary fee, a survey fee, a title search, a portion of the year's real estate taxes, and an attorney's fee. Is this depressing, or what? Excluding points you are likely to pay, these additional expenses may amount to from 3 to 5 percent of the purchase price of the home.

Refinancing

You may discover that a fall in the interest rates available on home loans has made it worthwhile to consider refinancing your old loan. Refinancing involves taking out a new loan and using all or part of the proceeds to pay off the remaining balance on the old loan. The goal of refinancing is to reduce the cost of living in your home by reducing the monthly interest you must pay. In fact, you may decide to extend the length of your mortgage by taking out a new loan that has a term that is longer than on your existing mortgage. On the other hand, you may decide to shorten the maturity of the new loan compared with the remaining life of the loan being refinanced. A lower interest rate will allow you to continue making the same payment as on the old loan while paying off the loan at an earlier date.

The drawback to refinancing a mortgage is paying the points and fees that are likely to be charged by the lender. You will probably have to pay several thousand dollars in up-front costs. You may again have to pay points in addition to a loan origination fee, notary fees, and so forth. These fees must be paid, even though it may not have been long since you last paid the exact same fees! The costs you are likely to incur in a mortgage refinancing are illustrated in Figure 39.

To determine if it is worthwhile to refinance, follow these steps:

1. Estimate the total fees and points you will have to pay. The lender will be able to provide this information.

2. Determine the payment reduction that results from the lower interest rate.

Tip

You can save tens of thousands of dollars in interest by shopping for the shortest-term mortgage with payments you can afford. Choosing a 15- or 20-year loan rather than a 25- or 30-year loan will result in forced savings in the form of higher monthly payments. The shorter-term loan, in turn, will produce tremendous total interest savings.

Figure 39 ■ The Costs of Refinancing a Home Loan

Refinancing costs vary significantly from lender to lender and from region to region. The following are estimates of what you might encounter in the event you decide to refinance your home. The lender that holds the current mortgage may be willing to reduce or forgo some of these fees, especially if your loan is relatively new and the title search, surveys, and inspections are still current. The cost of refinancing is likely to be substantially higher if the current mortgage contract contains a prepayment penalty. Depending on how much equity you have in the home, you may also be required to pay for mortgage insurance.

Application fee	$150	to	$250
Appraisal fee	$250	to	$350
Survey costs	$125	to	$300
Lender's attorney's fees	$250	to	$350
Title search and title insurance	$450	to	$600
Home inspection fees	$250	to	$350
Loan origination fees	1% of loan amount		
Points	1 to 3% of loan amount		

3. Multiply your (income) tax rate by the payment reduction calculated in step 2. Subtract the result from the payment reduction in step 2 in order to adjust for the reduction in tax deductions caused by a lower interest expense.

4. Calculate how long it will take to recover the closing costs by dividing the after-tax reduction in payments from step 3 into the closing costs determined in step 1.

Suppose 10 years ago you took out a 25-year mortgage that now has a balance of $80,000. Your top income is currently taxed at a rate of 25 percent. The existing loan has an 8 percent interest rate that requires monthly payments of $734. Interest rates have declined in the 10 years since you obtained the current loan, and a loan officer at the local financial institution indicates you can refinance your existing loan at the current market rate of 6.5 percent. The loan officer estimates that points and fees will amount to $3,200, and that the monthly payment on your new loan will be $596. The total time required to recover the costs of refinancing is $3,200 divided by the difference in payments ($734 − $596 = $138) minus 0.25 times the difference in payments ($138 × 0.25 = $34.50; $138 − $34.50 = $103.50), or 31 months ($3,200 ÷ $103.50 = 31). In other words, you will recover the cost of refinancing in less than three years. Monthly savings that continue beyond 31 months will be money in your pocket.

The less time required to recover the points and fees you must pay to obtain a new loan, the greater the incentive for refinancing. In general, you should consider refinancing a mortgage when you can recover all the costs within three or four years. You should not refinance when the period required to recover the refinancing fees exceeds the time you plan to live in the home. If you are fortunate enough to locate a lender who will refinance your loan without charging any points or fees, it will pay to refinance as frequently as you are able to obtain an interest rate lower than the rate on your current loan.

Once in a Lifetime: The Reverse Mortgage

Seniors who own their own home outright (i.e., there is no outstanding mortgage) have access to a potential source of cash in an unusual arrangement termed a *reverse mortgage.* Generally of interest to retirees in need of cash to meet living expenses, a reverse mortgage offers an opportunity to use the home as collateral for a loan in which the lender pays the borrower a series of tax-free cash flows. This is the reverse (hence, the name) of an ordinary mortgage, in which the borrower makes monthly payments to a lender until the loan is fully repaid. In a reverse mortgage the size of the mortgage grows ever larger as the lender makes a series of monthly payments to the borrower, generally for the borrower's lifetime. Principal and interest on the reverse mortgage are not due until the borrower dies, the home is sold, or the borrower moves out of the home for longer than 12 months. The lender gets a lien on the home, to which the borrower retains title and ownership. These mortgages typically have a variable interest rate that can change monthly or annually. Interest accrues and is added to the principal borrowed to determine the amount owed on the loan.

Like most financial products, reverse mortgages have a negative side. First, a reverse mortgage generally entails considerable expenses for the borrower, including mortgage insurance, origination fees, title insurance, an appraisal, and a monthly service charge. In addition, the mortgage means the home will pass to heirs with a debt attached. This may or may not be important. The initial expenses incurred by the borrower mean a reverse mortgage should be considered only when the borrower expects to draw payments over a considerable number of years. This type of mortgage is particularly suited to retirees who require extra cash to meet living expenses when the home is their main asset.

Glossary

acceleration clause A loan provision that allows a creditor to demand payment in full when a borrower fails to satisfy the terms of a loan agreement.

add-on clause A loan provision that allows new purchases to be added to an existing loan agreement.

adjustable-rate loan (ARM) A loan on which the applicable interest rate fluctuates according to a target interest rate or index of interest rates. Also called a variable-rate loan.

annual percentage rate (APR) The cost of credit expressed as an annual percentage of the amount owed. A standardized method of calculation makes the APR useful in comparing the interest cost of different loans.

average daily balance The sum of the outstanding credit card balances owed each day during the billing period divided by the number of days in the period.

balloon clause A clause in a loan agreement that requires a final payment substantially larger than previous payments.

bankruptcy A legal proceeding whereby a person unable to pay his or her debts in full may be discharged from the obligation to do so.

billing date On a credit card account, the last date of each month's statement on which transactions are reported. Also called *closing date.*

cash advance Cash obtained by a charge to a charge card or debit card.

cash value Savings that have accumulated in a life insurance policy and can be borrowed by the policyholder.

closed-end credit A one-time loan with specified payments and a predetermined maturity.

closing costs Expenses paid at settlement on a mortgage loan that include discount points, title insurance, escrow fees, attorney fees, recording fees, appraisal fees, notary fee, and so forth.

closing date See *billing date.*

collateral Assets pledged as security for a loan.

compound interest Interest that is calculated on interest from previous periods as well as on principal.

conditional sales contract A loan agreement in which title to the underlying property does not pass to the buyer until the last installment payment is made.

Consumer Credit Counseling Service A nonprofit organization that provides credit counseling services for individuals and families with serious financial problems.

Consumer Credit Protection Act See *Truth in Lending Act.*

Consumer Credit Reporting Reform Act A federal act that regulates the use of credit reports.

conventional loan A mortgage loan other than one that is insured or guaranteed by a government agency such as the FHA or VA.

conversion Changing an adjustable-rate mortgage to a fixed-rate mortgage.

cosigner A person who agrees to keep a loan current if the borrower does not.

credit agreement A contract between a borrower and a lender.

credit bureau A private business that gathers and distributes information regarding credit histories of consumers. Also called *credit reporting agency.*

credit history A person's credit record.

credit insurance Life insurance that repays your loan in the event of your death or disability.

creditor A person or business that lends money.

credit rating A creditor's judgment regarding the likelihood you will meet your credit obligations in a timely manner.

credit reporting agency See *credit bureau.*

credit risk The possibility a loan will not be fully repaid.

credit scoring A mathematical method for measuring someone's creditworthiness according to established relationships among income, outstanding debt, existing credit availability, and so forth.

debit card A plastic card that allows you to pay for purchases with funds that are immediately transferred from a financial account.

debt consolidation Replacing several smaller loans that have different maturities and interest rates with a single large loan, generally one that has a longer maturity.

default Failure to live up to the terms of a contract.

discount loan A loan on which the total amount of the finance charge is deducted in advance from the loan proceeds.

down payment The initial payment on a credit purchase. The down payment reduces a borrower's finance charges and protects a lender's position in the event the borrower defaults.

due date The date on which a loan payment is due.

Equal Credit Opportunity Act A federal act that bans discrimination in the extension of credit on the basis of age, color, sex, marital status, or race.

escrow A reserve account to take care of your real estate taxes and home insurance premiums when they come due.

Fair Credit Billing Act A federal act that establishes procedures for correcting billing mistakes, refusing to make payments on defective goods, and promptly crediting payments.

finance charge The total dollar amount you pay to use credit. The finance charge includes interest, service and transaction fees, premiums paid for credit life insurance, and so forth.

fixed interest rate A constant interest rate charged on a loan.

grace period On a credit statement, the number of days between the billing date and the due date. A longer grace period works to the favor of the borrower.

home-equity loan A loan that uses the equity in your home as collateral.

inflation A general increase in the price level of goods and services.

installment loan A loan with equal periodic payments.

interest A periodic charge for the use of credit.

interest rate The cost of borrowing money expressed as a percentage.

lien The legal right of a creditor to hold or sell property for payment of a claim.

line of credit The maximum amount of credit a lender will extend to a borrower during a specified period of time.

loan origination fee A lender's charge for evaluating and preparing a loan, generally applied to a mortgage loan.

loan qualification Determining whether a potential borrower can manage the required payments on a loan.

lock-in A lender's guarantee concerning the interest rate and fees on a loan.

margin account A brokerage account that allows the account holder to purchase securities on credit. With a margin account, one can also borrow against securities held in the account.

maturity date The date on which a loan is to be fully repaid.

minimum payment The minimum amount that you must pay (usually monthly) on your account.

mortgage loan A loan to purchase real estate that serves as collateral for the loan.

negative amortization An increase in the outstanding balance on a loan because payments made by the borrower are less than periodic interest charges.

net worth The value of assets that are owned, reduced by the amount of debts that are owed.

note A written promise to pay a specific amount of money on a certain date.

open-end credit A loan agreement in which credit is continuously granted to a predetermined maximum, and the borrower is billed periodically to make partial or full payment.

outstanding Describing the amount of a loan that remains to be paid.

periodic rate The interest rate charged on a loan during a particular period of time, often monthly.

prepayment penalty The lender's charge for an early payoff of a loan.

prime rate The interest rate commercial banks charge their most creditworthy customers. The prime rate influences the interest rate charged on many consumer loans.

principal The balance of a debt, excluding interest.

private mortgage insurance (PMI) Insurance that protects the lender against a loss in the event the borrower defaults on the loan.

refinance Revise a loan's payment schedule to extend payments or reduce interest.

repossession A borrower's surrender of an asset when the terms of a loan agreement have not been met.

rule of 78s A mathematical formula to determine how much interest has been paid on a loan at any point in time.

second mortgage A real estate loan over and above another loan that uses the same real estate as collateral.

secured credit card A credit card secured by funds deposited in a financial institution. Secured cards are designed for individuals who are unable to obtain a regular credit card.

secured note A loan agreement that includes the pledge of an asset that can be claimed by the creditor in the event the borrower fails to meet the terms of the agreement.

security interest A lender's control over property.

simple interest Interest calculated on principal only.

term The length of time between the signing of a loan agreement and when the loan is to be completely repaid.

Truth in Lending Act A federal law that requires disclosure of the annual percentage rate and the finance charges on a lending agreement. Also called *Consumer Credit Protection Act*.

unsecured note A lending agreement for which no specific assets are pledged by the borrower. The borrower's promise is the only guarantee of repayment.

usury laws State laws regulating interest rates that can be charged by creditors.

variable-rate loan See *adjustable-rate loan*.

Index

About the Author

David L. Scott has taught finance and investments at the college and university level for over thirty years. During this period he has conducted workshops, written numerous articles, and authored nearly two dozen books on business finance, personal finance, and investing. He has been a guest on numerous radio shows and appeared on NBC's *Today* and on CNBC. Dr. Scott was born in Rushville, Indiana, and received degrees from Purdue University and Florida State University before earning a PhD in economics from the University of Arkansas.